4.35

GW00674640

A Book of
RUSSIAN IDIOMS
Illustrated

A Book of
RUSSIAN IDIOMS
Illustrated

M. I. Dubrovin

Drawings By
V. I. Tilman

PERGAMON PRESS

OXFORD · NEW YORK · TORONTO
SYDNEY · PARIS · FRANKFURT

U.K.	Pergamon Press Ltd., Headington Hill Hall, Oxford OX3 0BW, England
U.S.A.	Pergamon Press Inc., Maxwell House, Fairview Park, Elmsford, New York 10523, U.S.A.
CANADA	Pergamon Press Canada Ltd., Suite 104, 150 Consumers Rd., Willowdale, Ontario M2J 1P9, Canada
AUSTRALIA	Pergamon Press (Aust.) Pty. Ltd., P.O. Box 544, Potts Point, N.S.W. 2011, Australia
FRANCE	Pergamon Press SARL, 24 rue des Ecoles, 75240 Paris, Cedex 05, France
FEDERAL REPUBLIC OF GERMANY	Pergamon Press GmbH, 6242 Kronberg-Taunus, Hammerweg 6, Federal Republic of Germany

Copyright © 1980 "Russky yazyk" Publishers

This edition 1981

British Library Cataloguing in Publication Data
Dubrovin, M
A Book of Russian Idioms Illustrated
1. Russian language - Conversation and phrase books
I. Title
491.7'8'3421   PG2689   79-40433
ISBN 0-08-023594-8

Made in Great Britain

PREFACE

The Russian language is highly idiomatic. The idioms, part and parcel of the language, add immensely to its richness. Their variety is accounted for by the historical development of the Russian language. More often than not Russian idioms are a stumbling block for non-Russian speakers, as they fail to understand Russian, both written and spoken, without the mastery of a sufficient number of idioms, especially those which occur most frequently.

This book is intended primarily for English speaking students of Russian who have a knowledge of the essentials of Russian grammar and are familiar with a basic Russian vocabulary.

The two types of idioms are mainly given in the book: **phraseological fusions,** word combinations whose meaning cannot be derived from the meaning of their elements (e.g. *собаку съел, заморить червячка*), and **phraseological unities,** word combinations whose meaning is partially dependent on the meaning of their individual words (e.g. *два сапога пара, капля в море*).

The idioms are arranged alphabetically as units. If the main verb can be used both in the imperfective and perfective aspects, the idiom is given in the aspect that occurs more frequently in speech. Idioms in which the order of components is not fixed strictly are given in their most typical form.

Each entry consists of a Russian idiom, its transliteration, literal translation and explanation. Also included wherever they were available, are English equivalents. (Given in many instances are two or three English idioms covering the meaning of the Russian idiom).

The literal translation method wants two explanations. First, 5 it was sometimes impossible to stick strictly to a word for word translation without making it sound like nonsense. When this is the case additional words were added to the English translations to make them sound more or less comprehensible (see, for example, *водой не разольёшь*). Also with that end in view the words *something* or *someone* were often added to the English translation.

Second, we are fully aware that any idiom literally translated into another language immediately loses its idiomatic force and very often presents a most awkward appearance. Moreover it is evident that the more an idiom gets rid of a direct reference to the literal meaning of its components the more it assumes the nature of a real idiom.

Still we believe that if the student knows what the components of the idiom mean, he will often find it easier to understand the meaning of the idiom.

A number of Russian idioms included in the book have more than one meaning. In this case given is the meaning that is more frequent in conversation.

Each entry, as a rule, is supplied with two pictures, one wherever possible to illustrate the literal meaning of the idiom, and the other to illustrate its real meaning. We hope that while the first picture can help convey the literal meaning of the idiom, or in other words, present its components, the second picture will show how the idiom behaves, i. e. in what circumstances it could be used. It should be borne in mind, however, that sometimes a number of synonymous meanings are given to explain the idiom, whereas the situational illustration refers to only one, which is the commonest.

The use of humorous drawings in this book is, in our view, justified by the fact that there is much humour in Russian idioms. Besides, the situational drawings give the idioms the emotional colouring that is characteristic of their usage in speech.

Russian idioms are largely of popular origin: hence their subject-matter is human life, or, better to say, human relations. In this respect we would like to point out that the word *душа* (*soul*), which is a component of many Russian idioms, does not have any mystic sense. This can be seen from the fact that in most cases the word *душа* can be and very often is replaced by the word *сердце* (*heart*) without changing the meaning of the idiom (e. g. *открывать душу /сердце, брать за сердце/ душу*, etc.). That is why a symbolic drawing of the human heart was given to represent the word *душа*.

Finally, we would like to say that although this book is something like a dictionary, it is not intended for use only as such. To be sure, that is one of its functions, but its overall purpose goes beyond this. We hope that the reader will find it interesting enough to use it not only for looking up one or another idiom that needs explaining. He will also find it a good companion that will help him get a taste of the peculiar charm and vividness that idioms lend Russian speech. Only if used in this way will the book have justified the work that has been put into it.

In this edition a few pictures were improved and about thirty new English equivalents of Russian idioms were included.

As far as we know this kind of book is the first attempt to present Russian idioms for foreign students in such a peculiar manner; therefore any criticism concerning the whole book or any aspect of it will be welcome.

Transliteration symbols to designate some difficult letters and combinations of letters in a Russian word

го at the end = vo

е, ё, ю, я after a vowel, **ь, ъ** and in the beginning = ye, yo, yu, ya

е, ё, ю, я after a consonant = 'e, 'o. 'u. 'a

ж = zh

ий, ый at the end = y

й after a vowel = y

ой = oy

тся = tsa

ться = ttsa

х = kh

ц = ts

щ = shch

ы after a consonant = y

ь after a consonant = '

LIST OF IDIOMS

1. Бабушка надвое сказала.
2. Бежать высунув язык.
3. Без сучка без задоринки.
4. Белая ворона.
5. Бить в одну точку.
6. Бить ключом.
7. Биться как рыба об лёд.
8. Блуждать в потёмках.
9. Больное место.
10. Больной вопрос.
11. Бояться собственной тени.
12. Брать кого-либо за сердце / душу.
13. Брать кого-либо под крылышко.
14. Брать с потолка.
15. Браться за ум.
16. Бросать камешки в чей-либо огород.
17. Бросать слова на ветер.
18. Бросаться кому-либо в глаза.
19. Бросаться словами.
20. Бросить тень на кого-либо / что-либо.
21. Быть между молотом и наковальней.
22. Быть на голову выше.
23. Быть на дружеской ноге.
24. Быть на ножах.
25. Быть на седьмом небе.
26. Быть не в своей тарелке.
27. Быть не из робкого десятка.
28. Быть не ко двору.
29. Быть не на своём месте.
30. Быть одетым с иголочки.
31. Быть у кого-либо под башмаком.
32. Быть связанным своим словом.
33. Валить в одну кучу.
34. Валить с больной головы на здоровую.
35. Валиться из рук.
36. Вариться в собственном соку.
37. Вбивать в голову.
38. Вбивать клин между кем-либо.
39. Вертеться как белка в колесе.
40. Вертится у кого-либо на языке.
41. Вешать нос.
42. Взвешивать свои слова.

9

43. Вздохнуть свободно.
44. Взять быка за рога.
45. Взять голыми руками.
46. Взять себя в руки.
47. Взять слово.
48. Видеть кого-либо насквозь.
49. Видно как на ладони.
50. Видно птицу по полёту.
51. Вилами на воде писано.
52. Висеть в воздухе.
53. Висеть на волоске.
54. Висеть на телефоне.
55. Витать в облаках.
56. Вить верёвки из кого-либо.
57. Вкладывать душу во что-либо.
58. Влететь в копеечку.
59. Влюбиться по уши.
60. Вогнать кого-либо в краску.
61. Водить кого-либо за нос.
62. Водой не разольёшь.
63. Воды не замутит.
64. Войти в историю.
65. Войти в колею.
66. Войти в роль.
67. Волосы становятся дыбом.
68. Вот где собака зарыта.
69. Вписать новую страницу во что-либо.
70. В подмётки не годится кому-либо.
71. Врастать корнями.
72. Вставать с левой ноги.
73. Вставать с петухами.
74. Вставлять палки в колёса.
75. Встречать в штыки.
76. Вступить в строй.
77. В ус не дуть.
78. Выбивать у кого-либо почву из-под ног.
79. Выбить из колеи.
80. Выбить из седла.
81. Выбросить из головы.
82. Выводить кого-либо из себя.
83. Выводить из строя.
84. Выводить кого-либо на чистую воду.
85. Выеденного яйца не стоит.
86. Выйти из пелёнок.
87. Выйти из себя.
88. Выйти из строя.
89. Выйти сухим из воды.
90. Вылететь в трубу.
91. Вынести что-либо на своих плечах.
92. Выносить сор из избы.
93. Вырастать в чьих-либо глазах.
94. Вырвать что-либо с корнем.
95. Высосать что-либо из пальца.
96. Вытягиваться в струнку.
97. Гадать на кофейной гуще.
98. Гладить кого-либо по головке.

99. Гладить кого-либо против шерсти.
100. Глаза разбегаются.
101. Глаза разгорелись.
102. Говорить под руку.
103. Голова идёт кругом.
104. Голодный как волк.
105. Горит в руках.
106. Готов сквозь землю провалиться.
107. Гусей дразнить.
108. Давать кому-либо сдачи.
109. Дальше ехать некуда.
110. Два сапога пара.
111. Делать из мухи слона.
112. Делать погоду.
113. Делать что-либо с закрытыми глазами.
114. Делать что-либо спустя рукава.
115. Делить шкуру неубитого медведя.
116. Денег куры не клюют.
117. Держать в чёрном теле.
118. Держать камень за пазухой.
119. Держать нос по ветру.
120. Держать себя в руках.
121. Держать ухо востро.
122. Держать язык за зубами.
123. Держаться в тени.
124. Длинный язык.
125. Доводить до белого каления.
126. Долгая песня.
127. Достать из-под земли.
128. До упаду.
129. Доходить до чьих-либо ушей.
130. Дрожит как осиновый лист.
131. Душа нараспашку.
132. Душа не на месте.
133. Душа ушла в пятки.
134. Дырявая голова.
135. Есть ещё порох в пороховницах.
136. Ехать зайцем.
137. Ждать у моря погоды.
138. Жить душа в душу.
139. Жить как кошка с собакой.
140. Жить как на вулкане.
141. Жить на широкую ногу.
142. Жить припеваючи.
143. Заблудиться в трёх соснах.
144. Заварить кашу.
145. Заглядывать в душу.
146. Заговаривать зубы.
147. Задать перцу.
148. Задеть за живое.
149. Задирать нос.
150. Зайти в тупик.
151. Закинуть удочку.
152. Заколдованный круг.
153. Закрадываться в душу.
154. Закрывать на что-либо глаза.
155. Замести следы.
156. Замкнуться в себе.
157. Заморить червячка.
158. Зарубить на носу.
159. Заткнуть за пояс.

160. Звёзд с неба не хватает.
161. Зелёная улица.
162. Знать что-либо вдоль и поперёк.
163. Знать все ходы и выходы.
164. Знать как свои пять пальцев.
165. Знать меру.
166. Золотая середина.
167. Золотое дно.
168. Золотые руки.
169. Зондировать почву.
170. Играть первую скрипку.
171. Играть с огнём.
172. Идти в гору.
173. Идти в огонь и в воду.
174. Идти куда глаза глядят.
175. Идти на поводу.
176. Идти по чьим-либо стопам.
177. Идти против течения.
178. Излить душу.
179. Измерить кого-либо взглядом.
180. Из одного теста.
181. Из ряда вон выходящий.
182. Иметь вес.
183. Иметь голову на плечах.
184. Искать вчерашний день.
185. Искать / не найти днём с огнём.
186. Искать иголку в стоге сена.
187. Искры из глаз посыпались.
188. Испить чашу до дна.
189. Испортить всю музыку.

190. И ухом не ведёт.
191. Ищи ветра в поле.
192. Как аршин проглотил.
193. Как без рук.
194. Как в аптеке.
195. Как в воду глядел.
196. Как в воду опущенный.
197. Как ветром сдуло.
198. Как гора с плеч свалилась.
199. Как гром среди ясного неба.
200. Как дважды два четыре.
201. Как две капли воды.
202. Как за каменной стеной.
203. Как из-под земли вырос.
204. Как из рога изобилия.
205. Как корова языком слизала.
206. Как на иголках.
207. Как небо от земли.
208. Как об стенку горох.
209. Как по маслу.
210. Как по нотам разыграть.
211. Как рукой сняло.
212. Как рыба в воде.
213. Как с гуся вода.
214. Как сельдей в бочке.
215. Как сквозь землю провалился.
216. Как снег на голову.
217. Как чёрт от ладана.
218. Камень на сердце.
219. Камень с души свалился.
220. Камня на камне не оставить.
221. Капля в море.
222. Кататься как сыр в масле.

223. Катиться под гору.
224. Каши не сваришь с кем-либо.
225. Кидает в жар.
226. Клевать носом.
227. Клин клином вышибать.
228. Когда рак свистнет.
229. Кот наплакал.
230. Кошки скребут на душе.
231. Краеугольный камень.
232. Красивый жест.
233. Красный как рак.
234. Крепкий орешек.
235. Кричать о чём-либо на всех перекрёстках.
236. Кровь с молоком.
237. Кто в лес, кто по дрова.
238. Куда ветер дует.
239. Купить кота в мешке.
240. Курам на смех.
241. Кусать себе локти.
242. Лёгкая рука.
243. Лёгок на подъём.
244. Лёд тронулся.
245. Лезть в бутылку.
246. Лезть в душу.
247. Лезть из кожи вон.
248. Лить воду на чью-либо мельницу.
249. Лить как из ведра.
250. Лить крокодиловы слёзы.
251. Ловить на лету.
252. Ловить кого-либо на слове.
253. Ловить рыбу в мутной воде.

254. Ломать голову над чем-либо.
255. Ломать копья.
256. Ломиться в открытую дверь.
257. Лопнуть как мыльный пузырь.
258. Мастер на все руки.
259. Махнуть рукой.
260. Медведь на ухо наступил.
261. Медвежья услуга.
262. Менять кукушку на ястреба.
263. Мерить на свой аршин.
264. Метать громы и молнии.
265. Мир тесен.
266. Много воды утекло.
267. Море по колено.
268. Мотать себе на ус.
269. Моя хата с краю.
270. Мурашки бегают по спине.
271. Мутить воду.
272. Мухи не обидит.
273. Мышиная возня.
274. Набить руку.
275. Набрать в рот воды.
276. На вес золота.
277. Навострить лыжи.
278. Навострить уши.
279. Навязнуть в зубах.
280. Надеяться как на каменную гору.
281. Надуть губы.
282. Нажимать на все кнопки.
283. Нажимать на все педали.

284. Называть вещи своими именами.
285. Найти себя.
286. Наклеивать ярлыки.
287. На лбу написано.
288. Наломать дров.
289. Намылить шею.
290. Нанести удар из-за угла.
291. Напустить туману.
292. Насолить кому-либо.
293. Наступать кому-либо на пятки.
294. Находиться на точке замерзания.
295. Нашла коса на камень.
296. Не видать как своих ушей.
297. Не видеть дальше своего носа.
298. Не видеть леса за деревьями.
299. Не видеть света белого.
300. Не выходит из головы.
301. Не за горами.
302. Не лезть за словом в карман.
303. Нем как рыба.
304. Не мытьём, так катаньем.
305. Не находить себе места.
306. Не нюхать пороху.
307. Не от мира сего.
308. Не ударить в грязь лицом.
309. Не уметь двух слов связать.
310. Не фунт изюму.
311. Нечист на руку.

312. Не чуять ног под собой.
313. Ни два ни полтора.
314. Ни жив ни мёртв.
315. Ни за какие коврижки.
316. Ни кола ни двора.
317. Ни к селу ни к городу.
318. Ни на что не похоже.
319. Ни пуха ни пера!
320. Ни рыба ни мясо.
321. Нож острый.
322. Номер не пройдёт.
323. Носа не высунуть.
324. Носить воду решетом.
325. Нужен как прошлогодний снег.
326. Обвести вокруг пальца.
327. Обещать золотые горы.
328. Обивать пороги.
329. Обратиться не по адресу.
330. Один как перст.
331. Одна нога здесь, другая там.
332. Одного поля ягода.
333. Оказаться между двух огней.
334. Оказаться между небом и землёй.
335. Окатить холодной водой.
336. Окунуться с головой.
337. Опустить руки.
338. Оставить с носом.
339. Остаться на бобах.
340. Остаться у разбитого корыта.
341. Откладывать на чёрный день.

342. Открывать Америку.
343. Открывать кому-либо глаза на кого-либо / что-либо.
344. Открывать кому-либо душу / сердце.
345. Открывать свои карты.
346. Откуда сыр-бор загорелся.
347. Палец о палец не ударить.
348. Палка о двух концах.
349. Пальца в рот не клади.
350. Пальцем кого-либо не тронуть.
351. Пальчики оближешь.
352. Первая ласточка.
353. Перегибать палку.
354. Переливать из пустого в порожнее.
355. Переломить себя.
356. Перемывать косточки.
357. Переполнить чашу терпения.
358. Песенка спета.
359. Писать как курица лапой.
360. Плавать как топор.
361. Плакаться в жилетку.
362. Платить той же монетой.
363. Плевать в потолок.
364. Плестись как черепаха.
365. Плыть по течению.
366. Побывать в чьей-либо шкуре.
367. Погнаться за двумя зайцами.
368. По горячим следам.
369. Подвернуться под руку.
370. Подвести кого-либо под монастырь.
371. Подводные камни.
372. Под горячую руку.
373. Поджать хвост.
374. Подлить масла в огонь.
375. Подложить свинью.
376. Поднести пилюлю.
377. Поднимать на щит.
378. Под носом.
379. Поднять всех на ноги.
380. Подписываться под чем-либо обеими руками.
381. Подрезать кому-либо крылья.
382. Под сурдинку.
383. Пожинать плоды.
384. Поймать на удочку.
385. Показать, где раки зимуют.
386. Показать когти.
387. Показать пятки.
388. Показывать товар лицом.
389. Полная чаша.
390. Положа руку на сердце.
391. Положить зубы на полку.
392. Положить кого-либо на обе лопатки.
393. Положить что-либо под сукно.
394. Попадаться кому-либо на язык.
395. По пальцам можно сосчитать.
396. Попасть в переплёт.

397. Попасть в точку.
398. Попасть как кур во щи.
399. Попасть кому-либо на зубок.
400. Попасть не в бровь, а в глаз.
401. Попасть пальцем в небо.
402. Попасться на чью-либо удочку.
403. Пороху не выдумает.
404. Пороху не хватает.
405. Посадить кого-либо в галошу.
406. Последний крик моды.
407. Последняя капля.
408. Последняя спица в колеснице.
409. После дождичка в четверг.
410. Поставить вопрос ребром.
411. Поставить всё на карту.
412. Поставить кого-либо в тупик.
413. Поставить крест на ком-либо / чём-либо.
414. Поставить кого-либо на своё место.
415. Почивать на лаврах.
416. Прибирать к рукам.
417. Привести кого-либо в себя.
418. Приложить руку к чему-либо.
419. Принимать за чистую монету.
420. Припирать кого-либо к стенке.

421. Притянуть что-либо за уши.
422. Пробный шар.
423. Провалиться с треском.
424. Проглотить пилюлю.
425. Проглотить язык.
426. Прожужжать все уши.
427. Пройти красной нитью.
428. Пройти сквозь огонь и воду.
429. Пройтись по чьему-либо адресу.
430. Пропускать мимо ушей.
431. Прятать концы в воду.
432. Птичьего молока не хватает.
433. Пуд соли съесть с кем-либо.
434. Пускать козла в огород.
435. Пускать кому-либо пыль в глаза.
436. Пушкой не прошибёшь.
437. Работать засучив рукава.
438. Работать не покладая рук.
439. Разбиваться в лепёшку.
440. Развесить уши.
441. Развязать кому-либо руки.
442. Развязать язык.
443. Разрядить атмосферу.
444. Расхлёбывать кашу.
445. Рвать и метать.
446. Рвать на себе волосы.
447. Рвать кого-либо на части.
448. Реветь белугой.
449. Родиться в сорочке.

450. Родиться под счастливой звездой.
451. Рубить сплеча.
452. Рубить сук, на котором сидишь.
453. Рука не дрогнет.
454. Рука не поднимается.
455. Руки коротки.
456. Руки не доходят.
457. Руки чешутся.
458. Рукой не достанешь.
459. Рыть яму кому-либо.
460. Садиться на любимого конька.
461. Садиться на шею.
462. Садиться не в свои сани.
463. Сами с усами.
464. Сапоги всмятку.
465. Сбрасывать маску.
466. Светлая голова.
467. Сводить концы с концами.
468. Своротить горы.
469. Связать кого-либо по рукам и ногам.
470. Сглаживать острые углы.
471. Сгорать со стыда.
472. Сгущать краски.
473. Сдавать в архив.
474. Семь потов сошло.
475. Семь пятниц на неделе.
476. Сердце / душа не лежит к чему-либо / кому-либо.
477. Сердце / душа разрывается на части.
478. Сесть в лужу.
479. Сесть на мель.
480. Сжечь корабли / мосты.
481. Сидеть между двух стульев.
482. Сидеть на чемоданах.
483. Сидеть сложа руки.
484. Склонять кого-либо во всех падежах.
485. Скользить по поверхности.
486. Сколько лет, сколько зим!
487. Слабая струнка.
488. С лёгким сердцем.
489. С лёгкой руки.
490. След простыл.
491. Сломать лёд.
492. С луны свалился.
493. Слышно, как муха пролетит.
494. Слюнки текут.
495. Сматывать удочки.
496. Смеяться в кулак.
497. Смотреть в корень.
498. Смотреть в оба.
499. Смотреть кому-либо в рот.
500. Смотреть другими глазами.
501. Смотреть как баран на новые ворота.
502. Смотреть сверху вниз.
503. Смотреть сквозь пальцы.
504. Смотреть сквозь розовые очки.
505. Снимать пенки.
506. Снимать с кого-либо стружку.

507. Снять перед кем-либо шляпу.
508. Собаку съел на чём-либо.
509. Совать нос во что-либо.
510. Сон в руку.
511. Сорить деньгами.
512. Со скрипом.
513. С открытой душой/с открытым сердцем.
514. Спать без задних ног.
515. С плеч долой.
516. Спутать все карты.
517. Сражаться с ветряными мельницами.
518. Ставить во главу угла.
519. Ставить кого-либо на ноги.
520. Ставить на одну доску.
521. Ставить что-либо с ног на голову.
522. Ставить точки над и.
523. Становиться на дыбы.
524. Старо как мир.
525. Стирать грани.
526. Стоит как вкопанный.
527. Стоять за кого-либо/что-либо горой.
528. Стоять над душой.
529. Стоять поперёк горла.
530. Стоять поперёк дороги.
531. Стреляный воробей.
532. Стрелять из пушки по воробьям.
533. Стричь всех под одну гребёнку.
534. Строить на песке.
535. С тяжёлым сердцем.
536. Считать ворон.
537. Сыт по горло.
538. Танцевать от печки.
539. Таскать каштаны из огня.
540. Тащить за уши.
541. Тёплое местечко.
542. Терять голову.
543. Терять почву под ногами.
544. Тише воды, ниже травы.
545. Толочь воду в ступе.
546. Трещать по швам.
547. Тяжёлая артиллерия.
548. Тяжёл на подъём.
549. Тянуть время.
550. Тянуть за язык.
551. Убить двух зайцев.
552. Ударить как обухом по голове.
553. Ударить по рукам.
554. Узнать что-либо из первых рук.
555. Уйти в кусты.
556. Уйти в себя.
557. Уйти с головой во что-либо.
558. Указать кому-либо на дверь.
559. Умывать руки.
560. Уносить ноги.
561. Упасть с неба на землю.
562. Устраивать сцену.
563. Утереть кому-либо нос.
564. Ухо режет.
565. Уши вянут.
566. Хватать звёзды с неба.
567. Хвататься за голову.

568. Хвататься за соломинку.
569. Ходить вокруг да около.
570. Ходить на голове.
571. Ходить по краю пропасти.
572. Ходить по струнке.
573. Хоть трава не расти.
574. Хоть шаром покати.
575. Хромать на обе ноги.
576. Худой как спичка.
577. Цены нет кому-либо / чему-либо.
578. Через чью-либо голову.
579. Через час по чайной ложке.
580. Чёрная кошка пробежала.
581. Чёрным по белому.
582. Чёртова дюжина.
583. Чесать язык.
584. Читать между строк.
585. Чудеса в решете.
586. Чужими руками жар загребать.
587. Шапками закидаем.
558. Шапочное знакомство.
589. Шито белыми нитками.
590. Шутки в сторону.
591. Яблоку негде упасть.
592. Язык сломаешь.
593. Язык хорошо подвешен.
594. Ясно как день.

РУССКИЙ АЛФАВИТ

А а [а]	**К к** [ка]	**Ц ц** [цэ]
Б б [бэ]	**Л л** [эль]	**Ч ч** [че]
В в [вэ]	**М м** [эм]	**Ш ш** [ша]
Г г [гэ]	**Н н** [эн]	**Щ щ** [ща]
Д д [дэ]	**О о** [о]	**Ъ ъ** [твёрдый
Е е [е]	**П п** [пэ]	знак]
Ё ё [ё]	**Р р** [эр]	**Ы ы** [ы]
Ж ж [жэ]	**С с** [эс]	**Ь ь** [мягкий
З з [зэ]	**Т т** [тэ]	знак]
И и [и]	**У у** [у]	**Э э** [э]
Й й [и	**Ф ф** [эф]	**Ю ю** [ю]
краткое]	**Х х** [ха]	**Я я** [я]

Б

1—32

1. **БАБУШКА НАДВОЕ СКАЗАЛА**

bábushka nádvoye skazála

Grandmother said it ambiguously.

It's very doubtful, undefined;
  it remains to be seen.

**Cf. We'll see what we'll see;
maybe rain or maybe snow, maybe yes or
maybe no.**

2. БЕЖАТЬ ВЫСУНУВ ЯЗЫК

b'ezhát' výsunuv yazýk

To run with one's tongue hanging out.

To run fast without
pausing for breath,
to be breathless from running.

**Cf. To run as fast as one's legs can
carry one; to run at a breakneck pace.**

3. БЕЗ СУЧКА БЕЗ ЗАДОРИНКИ

b'es suchká b'ez zadórinki

*Without a snag, without
any unevennes or roughness.*

Without any obstruction, difficulty
or complication; smoothly.

Cf. Without a hitch; like clockwork.

4. БЕЛАЯ ВОРОНА

b'élaya voróna

A white crow.

Someone unusual, extraordinary; not like others; an outsider.

Cf. Rara avis.

5. БИТЬ В ОДНУ ТОЧКУ

bit' v odnú tóchku

To keep striking the same spot.

To concentrate one's efforts on one thing in seeking to attain a specific goal.

6. БИТЬ КЛЮЧОМ

bit' kl'uchóm

To well up, to bubble.

To be in full operation; to proceed in a lively manner.

Cf. To boil over; to be in full swing.

7. БИТЬСЯ КАК РЫБА ОБ ЛЁД

bíttsa kak rýba ob l'ód

To beat against the ice like a fish.

To struggle desperately.

Cf. To pull the devil by the tail.

8. БЛУЖДАТЬ В ПОТЁМКАХ

bluzhdát' v pot'ómkakh

To grope in the dark.

To be without knowledge in some particular matter; to understand something vaguely; to act blindly.

Cf. To be in the dark about something.

9. БОЛЬНОЕ МЕСТО

bol'nóye m'ésto

A sore spot.

A matter that easily upsets one or about which one is sensitive; something that causes anxiety.

Cf. A sore / tender spot; a touchy subject.

10. БОЛЬНОЙ ВОПРОС

bol'nóy voprós

A sore question.

An urgent problem that is difficult to solve.

Cf. A sore point.

11. БОЯТЬСЯ СОБСТВЕННОЙ ТЕНИ

boyáttsa sóbstvennoi t'éni

To be afraid of one's own shadow.

To be unreasonably nervous due to groundless and trivial fears.

Cf. To be afraid of one's own shadow.

12. **БРАТЬ** кого-либо **ЗА СЕРДЦЕ/ДУШУ**

brat' zá s'ertse/dushu

To take someone by the heart/soul.

To excite, to move or touch deeply; to cause anxiety.

Cf. To pull at someone's heartstrings; to touch someone's heart.

13. **БРАТЬ** кого-либо **ПОД КРЫЛЫШКО**

brat' pod krýlyshko

To take someone under one's little wing.

To give someone every care and attention; to put someone under one's protection.

Cf. To take someone under one's wing.

27

14. БРАТЬ С ПОТОЛКА

brat' s potolká

To take something from the ceiling.

To allege
something without sufficient
factual grounds;
to say something without thinking,
at random.

**Cf. To make something up;
to talk through one's hat.**

15. БРАТЬСЯ ЗА УМ

bráttsa za úm

To take oneself by the mind.

To stop behaving imprudently;
to become sensible, reasonable.

Cf. To come to one's senses.

16. **БРОСАТЬ КАМЕШКИ В** чей-либо **ОГОРОД**

brosát' kám'eshki v ogoród

To throw pebbles into someone's kitchen-garden.

To allude to someone with mild derision;
to make an implied criticism.

Cf. To give someone a dig.

17. **БРОСАТЬ СЛОВА НА ВЕТЕР**

brosát' slová na v'ét'er

To throw words to the wind.

Not to care what
one says;
to speak at random
or idly.

**Cf. To talk
to the wind;
to waste one's breath.**

29

18. **БРОСАТЬСЯ** кому-либо **В ГЛАЗА**

brosáttsa v glazá

*To throw itself into
someone's eyes.*

To arrest attention, to be striking, to be conspicuous.

Cf. To catch someone's eye; to stare someone in the face.

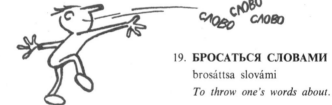

19. **БРОСАТЬСЯ СЛОВАМИ**

brosáttsa slovámi

To throw one's words about.

To speak irresponsibly, to use words lightly.

20. **БРОСИТЬ ТЕНЬ** на кого-либо/что-либо

brósit' t'en'

To cast a shadow on someone/something.

To put someone or
something in a bad
light; to cast suspicion
on someone; to blacken
someone's reputation.

**Cf. To cast a slur
on someone's
reputation.**

21. **БЫТЬ МЕЖДУ МОЛОТОМ И НАКОВАЛЬНЕЙ**

byt' m'ézhdu mólotom i nakovál'n'ey

*To be between the sledge-hammer
and the anvil.*

To be caught between two
equally serious evils or
dangers.

**Cf. To be between the
devil and the deep blue sea.**

31

22. БЫТЬ НА ГОЛОВУ ВЫШЕ

byt' ná golovu výshe

To be a head taller than someone.

To be far superior to someone (mentally or morally).

Cf. To be head and shoulders above someone.

23. БЫТЬ НА ДРУЖЕСКОЙ НОГЕ

byt' na drúzheskoy nog'é

To be on a friendly foot with someone.

To be on intimate or friendly terms with someone.

Cf. To be on a good/friendly footing with someone.

24. БЫТЬ НА НОЖАХ

byt' na nozhákh

To be on the knives.

To display mutual hostility.

**Cf. To be at daggers drawn;
to be at swords' points
with someone.**

25. БЫТЬ НА СЕДЬМОМ НЕБЕ

byt' na s'ed'móm n'éb'e

To be in the seventh heaven.

To be overfilled with joy, to be
supremely happy or satisfied.

**Cf. To tread/walk on air;
to be in seventh heaven.**

33

26. БЫТЬ НЕ В СВОЕЙ ТАРЕЛКЕ

byt' n'e v svoyéy tar'élk'e

To be not in one's personal plate.

To be not quite oneself,
to be not quite at ease,
to feel uneasy.

Cf. To be out of sorts.

27. БЫТЬ НЕ ИЗ РОБКОГО ДЕСЯТКА

byt' n'e iz róbkovo des'átka

To be not of the timid dozen.

Not one to scare easily; not easily frightened,
not a coward.

28. БЫТЬ НЕ КО ДВОРУ

byt' n'e ko dvorú

To be unfit for the courtyard.

To be unsuitable, to be
unwanted, not meeting
certain requirements;
to be an outsider.

Cf. Not to fit in.

29. БЫТЬ НЕ НА СВОЁМ МЕСТЕ

byt' n'e na svoyóm m'ést'e

To be not in one's own place.

To be unsuited to the
position one fills,
to be a misfit.
**Cf. A round peg
in a square hole.**

30. **БЫТЬ ОДЕТЫМ С ИГОЛОЧКИ**

byt' od'étym s igólochki

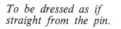

To be dressed as if straight from the pin.

To be dressed in a brand-new suit, dress, etc.

Cf. To be dressed up; as neat as a new pin.

31. **БЫТЬ** у кого-либо **ПОД БАШМАКОМ**

byt' pod bashmakóm

To be under someone's shoe.

To be under someone's predominant influence, to be in complete subjection (usually said of a man who is dominated by his wife).

Cf. To get someone by the short hairs; to be hen-pecked; to be under someone's thumb.

32. БЫТЬ СВЯЗАННЫМ СВОИМ СЛОВОМ

byt' sv'ázannym svoím slóvom

To be bound by one's word.

To be faithful in keeping one's promise.

B

33–96

33. ВАЛИТЬ В ОДНУ КУЧУ

valít' v odnú kúchu

To throw everything into one heap.

To put together, to mix up indiscriminately; to lump everything together.

34. ВАЛИТЬ С БОЛЬНОЙ ГОЛОВЫ НА ЗДОРОВУЮ

valít' s bol'nóy golový na zdoróvuyu

To shift something from an ailing head onto the one that doesn't ail.

To blame someone else
for one's own fault:

**Cf. To lay one's blame
at someone else's door;
to shift the blame on someone.**

35. ВАЛИТЬСЯ ИЗ РУК

valíttsa iz ruk

To fall out of one's hands.

Something doesn't go well because one is awkward, clumsy, doesn't feel like doing it, or doesn't have his heart in it.

36. ВАРИТЬСЯ В СОБСТВЕННОМ СОКУ

varíttsa v sóbstv'ennom sokú

To stew in one's own juice.

To keep solitary or apart from other people making no use of other people's knowledge and experience; to work solely by oneself without contact with others; to avoid social relations.

Cf. To be aloof; to keep to oneself.

37. ВБИВАТЬ В ГОЛОВУ

vbivát' v gólovu

To hammer something into someone's head.

To make something completely understood by emphatic repetition; to keep reiterating something to make it stick in someone's mind.

Cf. To hammer/drive something into someone's head.

38. **ВБИВАТЬ КЛИН** между кем-либо

vbivát' klin

To drive a wedge (between two groups of people or two individuals).

To cause a breach or separation, to split apart; to make people quarrel.

Cf. To drive a wedge.

39. **ВЕРТЕТЬСЯ КАК БЕЛКА В КОЛЕСЕ**

v'ert'éttsa kak b'élka v kol'es'é

To turn like a squirrel in a wheel.

To constantly busy oneself, to toil, to bustle about.

Cf. To be constantly on the go; to run/go around in small circles; to run around like a squirrel in a cage; to be busy as a bee/beaver.

41

40. **ВЕРТИТСЯ** у кого-либо **НА ЯЗЫКЕ**

v'értitsa na yazyk'é

It is whirling on someone's tongue.

On the verge of being uttered;
something at the back of one's
mind one wants to say but which
is not quite within recall of memory.

Cf. To be on the tip of one's tongue.

41. **ВЕШАТЬ НОС**

v'éshat' nos

To hang one's nose.

To be crest-fallen, discouraged,
despondent; to look dejected.

42. **ВЗВЕШИВАТЬ СВОИ СЛОВА**

vzv'éshivat' svoí slová

To weigh one's words.

To choose or use one's words with deliberation; to give something a comprehensive evaluation.

Cf. To weigh one's words.

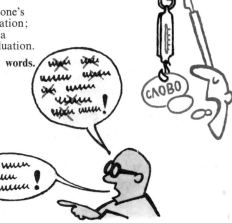

43. **ВЗДОХНУТЬ СВОБОДНО**

vzdokhnút' svobódno

To breathe freely.

To feel relieved of one's cares or troubles.

Cf. To give a sigh of relief.

44. ВЗЯТЬ БЫКА ЗА РОГА

vz'at' byká za rogá

To take the bull by the horns.

To take up a matter vigorously and promptly getting directly to its essence.

Cf. To take the bull by the horns.

45. ВЗЯТЬ ГОЛЫМИ РУКАМИ

vz'at' gólymi rukámi

To take someone or something with one's bare hands.

To seize, to take possession of someone or something without much difficulty, without making special effort.

Cf. Without a hand's turn; with one's bare hands.

46. ВЗЯТЬ СЕБЯ В РУКИ

vzyát' s'eb'á v rúki

To take oneself in one's hands.

To rouse oneself to renewed activity;
to make a determined effort, to regain
one's normal mental state, to regain
one's self-control.

**Cf. To take hold of oneself; to take oneself
in hand; to pull oneself together.**

47. ВЗЯТЬ СЛОВО

vz'at' slóvo

To take the word.

To rise to speak in a debate
at one's own request or initiative.

Cf. To take the floor.

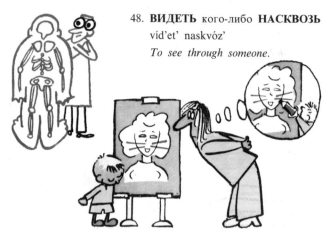

48. **ВИДЕТЬ** кого-либо **НАСКВОЗЬ**

víd'et' naskvóz'

To see through someone.

To know someone well; to be well aware of someone's thoughts and intentions.

Cf. To know someone inside out; to see through someone; to read someone like a book.

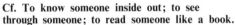

49. **ВИДНО КАК НА ЛАДОНИ**

vídno kak na ladóni

Seen as if it were on the palm of one's hand.

Spread before the eyes, in plain sight; easy to see or comprehend.

Cf. As plain as the nose on your face.

50. ВИДНО ПТИЦУ ПО ПОЛЁТУ

vídno ptítsu po pol'ótu

A bird is seen by its flight.

You can judge a person by his actions and behaviour.

51. ВИЛАМИ НА ВОДЕ ПИСАНО

vílami na vod'é písano

Written with a pitchfork on the water

It's uncertain, not defined, vague; it may or may not come off.

Cf. It's still all up in the air.

52. ВИСЕТЬ В ВОЗДУХЕ

vis'ét' v vózdukh'e

To be hanging in air.

To be undecided (said of a question or matter); to be in an uncertain position (said of a person).

Cf. To be in the air.

53. ВИСЕТЬ НА ВОЛОСКЕ

vis'ét' na volosk'é

To be hanging on a hair.

To be in a perilous state

Cf. To hang by a thread; to hang by a single hair.

54. ВИСЕТЬ НА ТЕЛЕФОНЕ

vis'ét' na t'el'efón'e

To be hanging on the telephone.

To talk incessantly on the telephone,
to spend hours on the telephone.

Cf. To sit on the phone.

55. ВИТАТЬ В ОБЛАКАХ

vitát' v oblakákh

To be hovering in the clouds.

To live in a dream world,
to indulge in day-dreams not
attending to everyday matters;
to let one's thoughts wander.

**Cf. To be up
in the clouds;
to go/be
wool-gathering.**

56. ВИТЬ ВЕРЁВКИ из кого-либо

vit' v'er'óvki

To plait ropes out of someone.

To have a strong influence on someone;
to have a person entirely
subservient to one's will.

**Cf. To twist someone
around one's little finger.**

57. ВКЛАДЫВАТЬ ДУШУ
во что-либо

vkládyvat' dúshu

To put one's soul into something.

To put all one's efforts into an
undertaking; to do something
whole-heartedly.

**Cf. To put one's heart
and soul into something.**

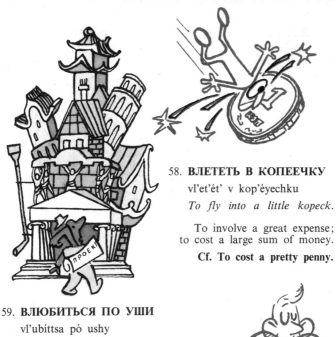

58. ВЛЕТЕТЬ В КОПЕЕЧКУ

vl'et'ét' v kop'éyechku

To fly into a little kopeck.

To involve a great expense;
to cost a large sum of money.

Cf. To cost a pretty penny.

59. ВЛЮБИТЬСЯ ПО УШИ

vl'ubíttsa pó ushy

To fall in love up to one's ears.

To be deeply enamoured of someone.

Cf. To be head over heels in love.

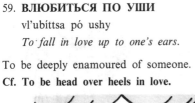

60. **ВОГНАТЬ** кого-либо **В КРАСКУ**

vognát' v krásku

To drive someone into the dye.

To cause someone to blush
from embarrassment.

Cf. To put someone to the blush.

61. **ВОДИТЬ** кого-либо **ЗА НОС**

vodít' zá nos

To lead someone by the nose.

To deceive, delude, mislead someone;
to make promises and not keep them.

**Cf. To make a fool of someone; to pull/draw
the wool over someone's eyes; to lead someone on.**

62. ВОДОЙ НЕ РАЗОЛЬЁШЬ

vodóy n'e razol'yósh

You couldn't split them apart with water.

To be very good friends, close to each other; inseparable from each other; to be always together.

Cf. As thick as thieves.

63. ВОДЫ НЕ ЗАМУТИТ

vodý n'e zamutít

He wouldn't muddy the water.

One who has extremely demure expression and manner; one who is quiet, meek, gentle.

Cf. He wouldn't hurt a fly; he looks as if butter wouldn't melt in his mouth.

64. ВОЙТИ В ИСТОРИЮ

voytí v istóriyu

To go down in history.

To become famous; to be remembered as a remarkable event.

Cf. To make history; to go down in history.

65. ВОЙТИ В КОЛЕЮ

voytí v kol'eyú

To get into the rut.

To return to one's habitual way of life;
to settle down into an ordinary way of life;
to get back into one's routine;
to return to normal.

Cf. To get into a groove.

66. ВОЙТИ В РОЛЬ

voytí v rol'

To enter into one's role.

To become securely and comfortably settled in a new job, position, occupation.

Cf. To begin to feel one's feet; to enter into one's role.

67. ВОЛОСЫ СТАНОВЯТСЯ ДЫБОМ

vólosy stanóv'atsa dýbom

One's hair stands on end.

One is struck with extreme horror.

Cf. One's hair stands on end.

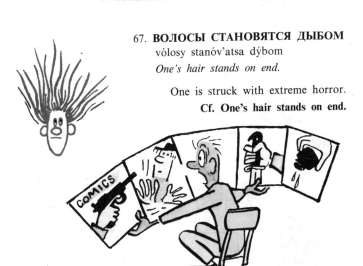

68. ВОТ ГДЕ СОБАКА ЗАРЫТА

vot gd'e sobáka zarýta

Here's where the dog is buried.

That's the main reason, the main point;
that's where the problem lies.

**Cf. That's the heart of the matter;
that's the crux of the matter.**

69. ВПИСАТЬ НОВУЮ СТРАНИЦУ
во что-либо

vpisát' nóvuyu stranítsu

To write a new page into something.

To make a discovery; to do something
outstanding, prominent in some field.

Cf. To add a fresh page to something.

70. В ПОДМЁТКИ НЕ ГОДИТСЯ
кому-либо

v podm'ótki n'e godítsa

Not fit to be soles of someone's shoes.

Someone or something is quite inferior to; not to be compared with, not nearly as good as.

Cf. Not fit to hold a candle to someone; to be not a patch on someone.

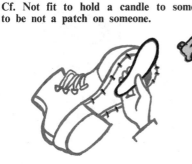

71. ВРАСТАТЬ КОРНЯМИ

vrastát' korn'ámi

To take root.

To become permanently and firmly established; to become attached to something; to get fully accustomed to something.

72. ВСТАВАТЬ С ЛЕВОЙ НОГИ

vstaváť s l'évoy nogí

To get up with one's left foot foremost.

To be in a bad or an irritable state of mind.

Cf. To get out of bed on the wrong side.

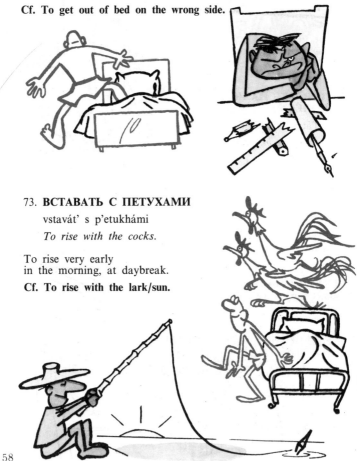

73. ВСТАВАТЬ С ПЕТУХАМИ

vstaváť s p'etukhámi

To rise with the cocks.

To rise very early
in the morning, at daybreak.

Cf. To rise with the lark/sun.

74. ВСТАВЛЯТЬ ПАЛКИ В КОЛЁСА

vstavl'át pálki v kol'ósa

To put sticks in the wheels.

To deliberately interfere
with the execution of a plan, operation, etc.

**Cf. To put a spoke in someone's wheel; to throw a spanner
in the works; to throw monkey wrenches in the machinery.**

75. ВСТРЕЧАТЬ В ШТЫКИ

vstr'echát' v shtykí

To meet someone or something with bayonets.

To give a hostile reception
to someone or something.

59

КОПЕРНИК

76. ВСТУПИТЬ В СТРОЙ

vstupít' v stroy

To step into formation.

To come into operation,
to become operative.

77. В УС НЕ ДУТЬ

v ús n'e dut'

Not to blow into one's moustache.

Not to care at all; not to show
any sign of emotion.

**Cf. Not to give a damn/a hang;
not to turn a hair.**

78. ВЫБИВАТЬ у кого-либо ПОЧВУ ИЗ-ПОД НОГ

vybivát' póchvu is-pod nog

To knock the ground from under someone's feet.

To deprive someone of his position or role in society;
to undermine somcone's confidence in something
completely; to disturb someone's peace of mind.

**Cf. To cut the ground from under someone's feet;
to take the wind out of someone's sails.**

79. ВЫБИТЬ ИЗ КОЛЕИ

výbit' is kol'eí

To kick someone out of the rut.

To upset someone's routine;
to unsettle someone.

Cf. To get someone out of the groove.

80. ВЫБИТЬ ИЗ СЕДЛА

výbit' is s'edlá

To knock someone out of the saddle.

To deprive someone of his position of control; to undermine someone's confidence in something completely; to disturb someone's peace of mind.

81. ВЫБРОСИТЬ ИЗ ГОЛОВЫ

výbrosit' iz golový

To throw something out of one's head.

To cause to forget; to dismiss from one's mind; to give up the idea.

Cf. To put something out of one's head.

82. **ВЫВОДИТЬ** кого-либо **ИЗ СЕБЯ**

vyvodít' is s'eb'á

To lead someone out of himself.

To exasperate, irritate someone.

**Cf. To drive someone out of his wits/mind;
to put someone beside himself.**

83. **ВЫВОДИТЬ ИЗ СТРОЯ**

vyvodít' is stróya

To take out of formation.

To disable something, to put
something out of operation.

84. **ВЫВОДИТЬ** кого-либо
НА ЧИСТУЮ ВОДУ

vyvodit' na chístuyu vódu

*To conduct someone
out onto pure water.*

To bring someone's misdeeds to light;
to expose someone.

**Cf. To show someone in his
true colours; to unmask.**

85. **ВЫЕДЕННОГО ЯЙЦА НЕ СТОИТ**

výyed'ennovo yaytsá n'e stóit

Not worth an empty egg-shell.

Entirely valueless, worth
nothing at all.

ЦЕНА

0,00001

ИЗОБРЕ-
ТЕНИЯ

**Cf. Not worth a rap/a
farthing/a hill of beans.**

86. ВЫЙТИ ИЗ ПЕЛЁНОК

výyti is p'el'ónok

To come out of one's swaddling-clothes.

To grow up, to become adult,
to be on one's own.

Cf. To be out of swaddling-clothes.

87. ВЫЙТИ ИЗ СЕБЯ

výyti is s'eb'á

To come out of oneself.

To be carried away
by excitement; to lose
control of oneself;
to be wrought up.

**Cf. To lose one's temper;
lo fly off the handle.**

88. ВЫЙТИ ИЗ СТРОЯ

výyti is stróya

To step out of formation.

To be disabled, to become unserviceable; to break down, to be put out of action.

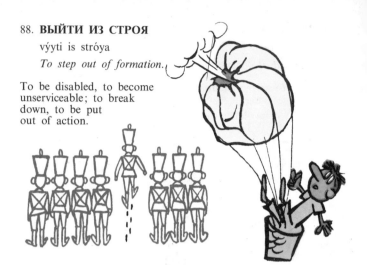

89. ВЫЙТИ СУХИМ ИЗ ВОДЫ

výyti sukhím iz vodý

To come out of the water dry.

To escape deserved punishment; to come out with one's reputation unblemished.

Cf. To come out unscathed; to get off scot-free.

90. ВЫЛЕТЕТЬ В ТРУБУ

výl'et'et' v trubú

To fly through the chimney.

To come to ruin financially, to go bankrupt; to have no money at all.

Cf. To go bust/smash.

91. ВЫНЕСТИ что-либо НА СВОИХ ПЛЕЧАХ

výnesti na svoíkh pl'echákh

To bear something on one's own shoulders.

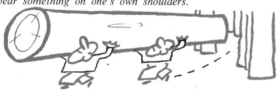

To take the whole burden of something; to endure the stress or strain of a difficult undertaking.

Cf. To bear the brunt of something.

92. ВЫНОСИТЬ СОР ИЗ ИЗБЫ

vynosít' sor iz izbý

*To carry the rubbish
out of one's hut.*

To let the outside world know about
one's private troubles, grievances, quarrels,
conduct that might be regarded
as disreputable; to utter abroad affairs
not meant for the public ear.

**Cf. To wash one's dirty linen in public;
to tell tales out of school.**

93. ВЫРАСТАТЬ В чьих-либо ГЛАЗАХ

vyrastát' v glazákh

To grow in someone's eyes.

To rise in someone's esteem;
to grow or improve
in someone's opinion.

94. ВЫРВАТЬ что-либо С КОРНЕМ

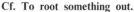

výrvat' s kórn'em

To tear something out with root.

To destroy something completely; to eradicate, to extirpate, to uproot something.

Cf. To root something out.

95. ВЫСОСАТЬ что-либо ИЗ ПАЛЬЦА

výsosat' is pál'tsa

To suck something out of one's finger.

To allege something which has no foundation in actual fact, absolutely groundless; to fabricate.

Cf. To make something up; to spin something out of thin air.

96. ВЫТЯГИВАТЬСЯ В СТРУНКУ

vyt'ágivattsa v strúnku

To stretch oneself into a string.

To stand stiffly erect;
to stand at attention.

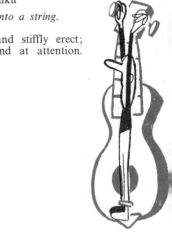

Г

97–107

97. **ГАДАТЬ НА КОФЕЙНОЙ ГУЩЕ**

gadát' na kofّéynoy gúshche

To tell fortunes by coffee ground.

To make groundless
statements;
to make wild
guesses.

**Cf. To tell someone's
fortune from the
tea-leaves in his cup.**

98. ГЛАДИТЬ кого-либо ПО ГОЛОВКЕ

gládit' po golóvk'e

To stroke someone's little head.

To show approval, to gratify; to show indulgence towards, to pander to someone.

Cf. To pat someone on the back.

99. ГЛАДИТЬ кого-либо ПРОТИВ ШЕРСТИ

gládit' prótiv shérsti

To stroke someone against his hair.

To do or say something contrary to someone's prejudices, opinions, or habits.

Cf. To rub/stroke someone the wrong way.

100. ГЛАЗА РАЗБЕГАЮТСЯ

glazá razb'egáyutsa

*One's eyes are running
in different directions.*

One doesn't know what to look at first;
one is dazzled by the sight of so many
things; one is unable to concentrate
on one thing.

101. ГЛАЗА РАЗГОРЕЛИСЬ

glazá razgor'élis'

One's eyes have lit up.

One desires something earnestly;
one is looking longingly
or desiringly at something.

Cf. To be dying for.

102. ГОВОРИТЬ ПОД РУКУ

govorít' pód ruku

To speak to someone's hand.

To say something at
the wrong time;
to disturb someone
when he is concentrating
on something; to distract
someone by talking.

Cf. To put someone off.

103. ГОЛОВА ИДЁТ КРУГОМ

golová id'ót krúgom

One's head is going round.

Someone has a lot to do, is in a state
of bewilderment or confusion being worn
out with troubles and worry.

**Cf. One's head is spinning; one's head is
in a whirl; one's head is going round and round.**

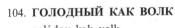

104. ГОЛОДНЫЙ КАК ВОЛК

golódny kak volk

Hungry as a wolf.

Terribly hungry.

Cf. Hungry as a hunter.

105. ГОРИТ В РУКАХ

gorít v rukákh

*It is burning
in one's hands.*

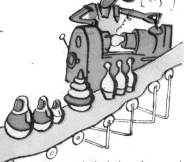

The work is being done quickly,
energetically, deftly;
the work is going fine.

**Cf. Someone has clever hands;
someone is working like lightning.** 75

106. ГОТОВ СКВОЗЬ ЗЕМЛЮ ПРОВАЛИТЬСЯ

gotóv skvoz' z'éml'u provalíttsa

Ready to fall through the ground.

One earnestly wishes to disappear; one feels so ashamed or embarrassed that he wishes that the earth would swallow him up.

Cf. He wishes the ground would open under him.

107. ГУСЕЙ ДРАЗНИТЬ

gus'éy draznít'

To tease the geese.

To irritate, to annoy someone (often without purpose or reason); to provoke ill feelings.

Д

108 – 134

108. **ДАВАТЬ** кому-либо **СДАЧИ**

   davát' zdáchi

   To give someone the change.

To retaliate as vigorously as one is attacked; to give as good as one got; to return insult for insult.

Cf. To answer in kind.

109. ДАЛЬШЕ ЕХАТЬ НЕКУДА

dál'she yékhat' n'ékuda

You can't go farther.

Things couldn't be worse; that's the end of it; that's the limit.

110. ДВА САПОГА ПАРА

dva sapogá pára

Two boots make a pair.

They are alike; (usually with reference to disposition, tastes, conduct, etc.); they are well matched; they deserve each other; one is no better than the other.

Cf. They make a pair; birds of one feather; not a pin to choose between them.

78

111. ДЕЛАТЬ ИЗ МУХИ СЛОНА

d'élat' iz múkhi sloná

To make an elephant out of a fly.

To exaggerate the importance of a small matter.

Cf. To make a mountain out of a molehill.

112. ДЕЛАТЬ ПОГОДУ

d'élat' pogódu

To make the weather.

To determine the course of events, to affect a matter directly; to have a dicisive influence on a matter.

79

113. ДЕЛАТЬ что-либо С ЗАКРЫТЫМИ ГЛАЗАМИ

d'élat' z zakrýtymi glazámi

To do something with one's eyes closed.

To do something without thinking, carelessly, rashly.

114. ДЕЛАТЬ что-либо СПУСТЯ РУКАВА

d'élat' spust'á rukavá

To do something with one's sleeves lowered.

To do something carelessly without paying attention to it;
to fail to tend properly to affairs;
to do something in a slipshod manner.

Cf. To let things slide.

115. ДЕЛИТЬ ШКУРУ НЕУБИТОГО МЕДВЕДЯ

d'elít' shkúru n'eubítovo m'edv'éd'a

To divide the skin of an unkilled bear.

To anticipate too confidently the possession of something that one may never receive; to make plans which depend on events that may not happen.

Cf. To count one's chickens before they are hatched; to sell the bear's skin before one has caught the bear.

116. ДЕНЕГ КУРЫ НЕ КЛЮЮТ

d'én'eg kúry n'e kl'uyút

The hens don't peck at the money.

One has plenty of money.

Cf. Rolling in money.

81

117. ДЕРЖАТЬ В ЧЁРНОМ ТЕЛЕ

d'erzhát' v chórnom t'él'e

To keep in a black body.

To ill-treat, to treat someone roughly; to hold in subjection.

118. ДЕРЖАТЬ КАМЕНЬ ЗА ПАЗУХОЙ

derzhát' kám'en' za pázukhoy

To keep a stone inside one's shirt.

To secretly bear a grudge against someone; to nurse a grievance; to harbour thoughts of revenge; to have evil intentions.

119. ДЕРЖАТЬ НОС ПО ВЕТРУ

d'erzhát' nos po v'étru

To keep one's nose to the wind.

To adapt to circumstances, unscrupulously altering one's convictions or behaviour; to adjust to the situation.

Cf. To trim one's sails to the wind.

120. ДЕРЖАТЬ СЕБЯ В РУКАХ

derzhát s'eb'á v rukákh

To keep oneself in one's hands.

To restrain oneself; to preserve one's self-control.

Cf. To hold/keep oneself in check; to keep oneself in hand.

83

121. ДЕРЖАТЬ УХО ВОСТРО

d'erzhát' úkho vostró

To keep one's ear sharp.

To behave circumspectly,
to act with caution;
to be on guard;
to mistrust someone.

**Cf. To watch one's step;
to be on the qui vive;
to keep one's eyes peeled.**

122. ДЕРЖАТЬ ЯЗЫК ЗА ЗУБАМИ

d'erzhát' yazýk za zubámi

To hold one's tongue behind one's teeth.

To keep silent, not to blab;
to be cautious in what one says.

**Cf. To hold one's tongue;
to keep one's breath
to cool one's porridge.**

123. **ДЕРЖАТЬСЯ В ТЕНИ**

d'erzháttsa v t'ení

To hold to the shade.

To behave so as to remain unnoticed.

Cf. To stay in the background.

124. **ДЛИННЫЙ ЯЗЫК**

dlínny yazýk

A long tongue.

Talkative, unable to hold one's tongue; a blabber.

Cf. To have a long tongue; to wag one's tongue.

125. ДОВОДИТЬ ДО БЕЛОГО КАЛЕНИЯ

dovodít' do b'élovo kal'éniya

To bring to a white heat.

To drive someone to a
frenzy, to infuriate,
to rouse to fury;
to make someone lose
his self-control.

126. ДОЛГАЯ ПЕСНЯ

dólgaya p'ésn'a

A long song.

Something that cannot be done
or explained quickly; something
that takes a long time to be
accomplished; a drawn out affair.

86 **Cf. A long story.**

127. ДОСТАТЬ ИЗ-ПОД ЗЕМЛИ

dostát' is-pod z'emlí

To get from under the ground.

To get something no matter how difficult.

Cf. To go to the end of the earth to get something.

128. ДО УПАДУ

do upádu

Till one falls down.

To the point of exhaustion, till one drops.

129. ДОХОДИТЬ ДО чьих-либо УШЕЙ

dokhodít' do ushéy

To come to someone's ears.

To become known to someone.

Cf. To reach someone's ears.

130. ДРОЖИТ КАК ОСИНОВЫЙ ЛИСТ

drozhít kak osínovy list

One shakes like an aspen leaf.

One trembles violently
(usually with excitement
or fear).

**Cf. To shake/quake
like an aspen leaf.**

131. ДУША НАРАСПАШКУ

dushá naraspáshky

One's soul is open (unbuttoned).

To be frank, sincere, candid, straightforward.

Cf. Open-hearted.

132. ДУША НЕ НА МЕСТЕ

dushá n'e na m'ést'e

One's soul is not in its place.

To be anxious; to feel uneasy.

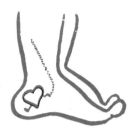

133. ДУША УШЛА В ПЯТКИ

duchá ushlá v p'átki

One's soul has gone into one's heels.

Someone is greatly alarmed by what is happening or anticipated to happen; terribly frightened.

Cf. One's heart sank into one's boots; to have one's heart in one's mouth.

134. ДЫРЯВАЯ ГОЛОВА

dyr'ávaya golová

A holey head.

Someone who has a very poor memory; someone who is forgetful, absent-minded.

Cf. To have a head like a sieve.

135. **ЕСТЬ ЕЩЁ ПОРОХ
В ПОРОХОВНИЦАХ**

yest' yeshcó pórokh
v porokhovnítsakh

*There is still some gunpowder
in the powder-flasks.*

Still full of vim and vigour;
still able to fight·or to
do something important.

Cf. We are not licked yet.

136. ЕХАТЬ ЗАЙЦЕМ

yékhat' záytsem

To ride as a hare.

To travel without paying
for a ticket.

137–142

137. ЖДАТЬ У МОРЯ ПОГОДЫ

zhdat' u mór'a pogódy

To wait by the sea for the weather.

To indulge in vain hopes without taking any steps to realize them; to waste one's time neglecting one's opportunities.

Cf. To let the grass grow under one's feet.

138. ЖИТЬ ДУША В ДУШУ

zhit' dushá v dúshu

To live soul and soul together.

To live in peace, harmony, concord or perfect amity with someone.

139. ЖИТЬ КАК КОШКА С СОБАКОЙ

zhit' kak kóshka s sobákoy

To live like a cat and a dog.

To be constantly snapping, bickering and quarrelling.

Cf. To fight like cats and dogs.

140. ЖИТЬ КАК НА ВУЛКАНЕ

zhit' kak na vulkán'e

To live as on a volcano.

To be in constant
anticipation of trouble.

**Cf. To sit on a powder-keg;
to be living on the edge of a volcano;
to be sitting on a volcano.**

141. ЖИТЬ НА ШИРОКУЮ НОГУ

zhit' na shirókuyu nógu

To live on a broad foot.

To live in luxury; to live sumptuously, sparing no expense.

Cf. To live like a lord; to live in grand style.

142. **ЖИТЬ ПРИПЕВАЮЧИ**

  zhit' prip'eváyuchi

  To live humming a tune.

To live in comfortable
circumstances; to live happily.

Cf. To be in clover.

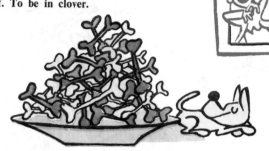

3

143–169

143. ЗАБЛУДИТЬСЯ В ТРЁХ СОСНАХ

zabludíttsa v tr'okh sósnakh

To lose one's way among three pines.

To fail to find a solution to a simple problem; to fail to comprehend something elementary.

Cf. To lose one's way in broad daylight.

$$a^2 = b^2 + c^2$$

144. ЗАВАРИТЬ КАШУ

zavarít' káshu

To cook kasha.

To start a complicated, risky or troublesome affair.

Cf. To stir up trouble; to make a mess of something.

---

* kasha — a dish of cooked grain or groats.

145. ЗАГЛЯДЫВАТЬ В ДУШУ

zagl'ádyvat' v dúshu

To peep into someone's soul.

To try to fathom someone's innermost thoughts; to try to find out what is in someone else's heart.

146. ЗАГОВАРИВАТЬ ЗУБЫ

zagovárivat' zúby

To talk someone's teeth.

To evade the issue with irrelevant talk.

Cf. To put someone off with fair words.

147. ЗАДАТЬ ПЕРЦУ

zadát' p'értsu

To give pepper.

To rate someone soundly and severely; to punish someone.

Cf. To give it hot to someone; to make it hot for someone.

148. ЗАДЕТЬ ЗА ЖИВОЕ
zad'ét' za zhivóye

To graze a raw place.

To excite greatly, to thrill; to stir someone's self-esteem or pride.

Cf. To cut/sting to the quick.

149. ЗАДИРАТЬ НОС
zadirát' nos

To lift up one's nose.

To act in a superior and affected manner; to become puffed up, conceited.

Cf. To turn up one's nose; to put on airs; to cock one's nose.

150. ЗАЙТИ В ТУПИК

zaytí v tupík

To come into a blind alley.

To find oneself
in a desperate position.

Cf. To reach a deadlock.

151. ЗАКИНУТЬ УДОЧКУ

zakínut' údochku

To cast a line.

To make an indirect reference to something
in order to find out more about it; to drop
a hint by way of suggestion.

**Cf. To put a line out; to put
forth/send out a feeler.**

152. ЗАКОЛДОВАННЫЙ КРУГ

zakoldóvanny krug

A bewitched circle.

A hopeless situation; a state of affairs from which it's difficult to find a way out.

Cf. A vicious circle.

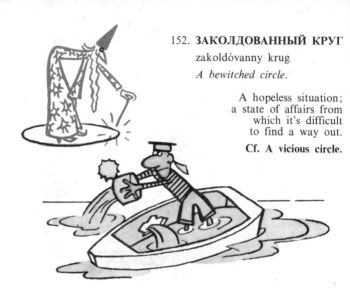

153. ЗАКРАДЫВАТЬСЯ В ДУШУ

zakrádyvattsa v dúshu

To creep into someone's soul.

To creep or steal into one's mind (said of thoughts or feelings).

154. **ЗАКРЫВАТЬ** на что-либо **ГЛАЗА**

zakryvát' glazá

To close one's eyes to something.

To ignore, deliberately not to pay attention to or recognize something (especially, improper conduct).

Cf. To close/shut one's eyes to something; to wink at something.

155. **ЗАМЕСТИ СЛЕДЫ**

zam'estí sl'edý

To sweep over one's traces.

To destroy something that can be used as evidence; to conceal one's movements or activities.

Cf. To cover up one's tracks/traces.

156. ЗАМКНУТЬСЯ В СЕБЕ

zamknúttsa v s'eb'é

To get locked up in one's own self.

To become less sociable and more reserved; to withdraw from the society of one's fellows; to retire into oneself.

**Cf. To shut oneself up;
to withdraw/retire into one's shell.**

157. ЗАМОРИТЬ ЧЕРВЯЧКА

zamorít' cherv'achká

To underfeed the little worm.

To have a little to eat.

**Cf. To have a snack; to have a bite;
to take the edge off one's hunger.**

158. ЗАРУБИТЬ НА НОСУ

zarubít' na nosú

To make a notch on one's nose.

To remember something firmly, forever.

**Cf. Bear it in mind;
put that into your pipe and smoke it.**

159. ЗАТКНУТЬ ЗА ПОЯС

zatknút' za póyas

To stick someone behind one's belt.

To surpass, to outstrip,
to outdo someone.

**Cf. To outshine someone;
to knock someone
into a cocked hat.**

160. ЗВЁЗД С НЕБА НЕ ХВАТАЕТ

zv'ozd s n'éba n'e khvatáyet

He/she doesn't snatch stars from the sky.

One isn't a remarkable person; one is a person of average or mediocre abilities.

Cf. He won't set the Thames/world on fire.

161. ЗЕЛЁНАЯ УЛИЦА

z'el'ónaya úlitsa

A green street.

An open thoroughfare; also used to indicate that there is nothing standing in one's way.

Cf. The green light.

162. ЗНАТЬ что-либо ВДОЛЬ И ПОПЕРЁК

znat' vdol' i pop'er'ók

To know something lengthwise and crosswise.

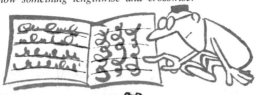

To know something
thoroughly in all its details.

**Cf. To know something
inside out.**

163. ЗНАТЬ ВСЕ ХОДЫ И ВЫХОДЫ

znat' vs'e khodý i výkhody

To know all the entrances and exits.

To know all the details or intricacies;
to be thoroughly familiar with what
is to be done under the circumstances.

**Cf. To know one's way around; to know
all the ins and outs; to know the ropes.**

164. ЗНАТЬ КАК СВОИ ПЯТЬ ПАЛЬЦЕВ

znat' kak svoyí p'at' pál'tsev

To know something as well as one's own five fingers.

To know something thoroughly; to be quite familiar with something.

Cf. To know something like the palm of one's hand.

165. ЗНАТЬ МЕРУ

znat' m'éru

To know the measure.

To know one's limits; to be moderate; to know when to stop.

166. ЗОЛОТАЯ СЕРЕДИНА

zolotáya s'er'edína

The golden middle.

The safe, prudent way between extremes; the principle of moderation.

Cf. The golden mean.

167. ЗОЛОТОЕ ДНО

zolotóye dno

A golden bottom.

An inexhaustible source of wealth.

Cf. A gold mine.

168. ЗОЛОТЫЕ РУКИ

zolotýye rúki

Golden hands.

A master of one's craft.

Cf. A clever pair of hands; skillful/deft fingers.

169. ЗОНДИРОВАТЬ ПОЧВУ

zondírovat' póchvu

To probe the ground.

To try cautiously to discover someone's inclinations, to test the views of others, to sound out one's chances of success beforehand.

Cf. To find out how the things stand; to explore the ground; to put forth/throw out a feeler.

И

170–191

170. **ИГРАТЬ ПЕРВУЮ СКРИПКУ**
igrát' pérvuyu skrípku
To play the first violin.

To play a leading role in some undertaking.

Cf. To play first fiddle.

171. ИГРАТЬ С ОГНЁМ

igrát' s ogn'óm

To play with fire.

To trifle with something likely to prove dangerous without considering the consequences.

Cf. To play with edge-tools; to play with fire.

172. ИДТИ В ГОРУ

ittí v góru

To go uphill.

To gain influence; to attain promotion; to make a prosperous career.

Cf. To go up/rise in the world; to climb up the ladder.

ДИРЕКТОР ЦИРКА

173. ИДТИ В ОГОНЬ И В ВОДУ

ittí v ogón' i v vódu

To go into fire and water.

To submit to any ordeal, to encounter or face the greatest dangers or hardest chances, to be ready to do anything for someone or something.

Cf. To go through fire and water.

174. ИДТИ КУДА ГЛАЗА ГЛЯДЯТ

ittí kudá glazá gl'ad'át

To walk wherever one's eyes are looking.

To wander aimlessly; to go wherever one's feet will carry one.

113

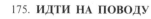

175. ИДТИ НА ПОВОДУ

itti na povodú

To walk on someone's rein.

To be dependent on someone.

**Cf. To be led by;
to be under someone's thumb.**

176. ИДТИ ПО чьим-либо СТОПАМ

itti po stopám

To walk in someone's footsteps.

To follow someone's example;
to be someone's disciple.

Cf. To follow in someone's footsteps.

177. **ИДТИ ПРОТИВ ТЕЧЕНИЯ**

itti prótiv t'echéniya

To go against the stream.

To act against the general trend of
thought, opinion, custom, etc.

**Cf. To go against
the tide/current/stream.**

178. **ИЗЛИТЬ ДУШУ**

izlít' dúshu

To pour out one's soul.

To relieve one's mind by talking about one's troubles.

**Cf. To unbosom oneself; to unburden one's heart;
to bare one's heart/soul.** 115

179. **ИЗМЕРИТЬ** кого-либо **ВЗГЛЯДОМ**

izm'érit' vzgl'ádom

To measure someone with one's glance.

To examine someone closely from head to toe.

Cf. To look someone up and down; to measure someone with one's eye.

180. **ИЗ ОДНОГО ТЕСТА**

iz odnovó t'ésta

Made of the same dough

They are just about the same in disposition, tastes, etc.

Cf. Two of a kind; the same breed; cut from the same cloth; birds of one feather.

181. ИЗ РЯДА ВОН ВЫХОДЯЩИЙ

iz r'áda von vykhod'áshchy
Going out of the line.

Outstanding, exceptional
out of the ordinary.

Cf. Out of the common run.

182. ИМЕТЬ ВЕС

im'ét' v'es
To have weight.

To be highly influential or important.

Cf. To carry a lot of weight.

183. ИМЕТЬ ГОЛОВУ НА ПЛЕЧАХ

im'ét' gólovu na pl'echákh

To have a head on one's shoulders.

To be intelligent and reasonable; to be able to think for oneself.

Cf. To have a good head on one's shoulders.

184. ИСКАТЬ ВЧЕРАШНИЙ ДЕНЬ

iskát' vcheráshny d'en'

To search for yesterday.

To waste time on a hopeless quest.

Cf. To go on a wild-goose chase.

185. ИСКАТЬ / НЕ НАЙТИ ДНЁМ С ОГНЁМ

iskát'/n'e naytí dn'om s ogn'óm

To search for someone or something by day with a light.

To seek in vain; to look hard for someone or something with little chance of finding; it's nowhere to be found.

Cf. You will not find it in a month of Sundays; you can't get it for love or money.

186. ИСКАТЬ ИГОЛКУ В СТОГЕ СЕНА

iskát' igólku v stóg'e s'éna

To look for a needle in a bundle of hay.

To look for something or someone virtually impossible to find.

Cf. To look for a needle in a haystack.

119

187. ИСКРЫ ИЗ ГЛАЗ ПОСЫПАЛИСЬ

ískry iz glaz posýpalis'

Sparks began to pour out of one's eyes.

A sensation of light flashing before one's eyes, caused by a blow in the face or on the head.

Cf. To see stars.

188. ИСПИТЬ ЧАШУ ДО ДНА

ispít' cháshu do dná

To drink the bowl to the bottom.

To experience ordeals, hardships, sorrows, misfortunes in full measure.

Cf. To drink/drain the cup (of bitterness, sorrow, etc.) to the dregs.

189. ИСПОРТИТЬ ВСЮ МУЗЫКУ

ispórtit' vs'u múzyku

To spoil all the music.

To upset a plan; to disrupt the procedure;
to cause disturbance.

**Cf. To upset someone's apple-cart;
to play the very devil with something.**

190. И УХОМ НЕ ВЕДЁТ

i úkhom n'e v'ed'ót

Doesn't wiggle an ear.

One doesn't pay the least attention to something; one
doesn't react at all; one deliberately shows indifference.

Cf. Without batting an eyelid.

191. **ИЩИ ВЕТРА В ПОЛЕ**

ishchí v'étra v pól'e

Look for the wind in the field.

It's gone without leaving a trace;
it's nowhere to be found and it can never be returned.

**Cf. To look for a needle in a haystack;
to go on a wild-goose chase.**

К

192–241

192. КАК АРШИН ПРОГЛОТИЛ

kak arshín proglotíl

As if one had swallowed an arshin*.

Unnaturally erect, quite stiff;
rigid, upright in bearing.

Cf. As stiff as a poker.

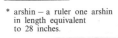

* arshin – a ruler one arshin
in length equivalent
to 28 inches.

193. КАК БЕЗ РУК

kak b'ez rúk

As if without the hands.

To feel quite helpless without something or someone.

194. КАК В АПТЕКЕ

kak v apt'ék'e

Just like at the chemist's.

Exactly, precisely; just so, just right.

Cf. To a T.

195. КАК В ВОДУ ГЛЯДЕЛ

kak v vódu gl'ad'él

Like having looked into the water.

As if something had
been known beforehand;
someone was able to foresee future events.

Cf. He must have second sight.

196. КАК В ВОДУ ОПУЩЕННЫЙ

kak v vódu opúshchenny

As if lowered into the water.

Dejected, downcast,
depressed, crest-fallen.

**Cf. To be down
in the chops/mouth.** 125

197. КАК ВЕТРОМ СДУЛО

kak v'étrom sdúlo

As if the wind blew it away.

Someone or something has rapidly
and mysteriously disappeared
without a trace.

Cf. To vanish into thin air.

198. КАК ГОРА С ПЛЕЧ СВАЛИЛАСЬ

kak gorá s pl'ech svalílas'

As if a mountain had fallen off one's shoulders.

Someone is relieved of anxiety, doubt, cares.

Cf. A load off one's mind.

126

199. КАК ГРОМ СРЕДИ ЯСНОГО НЕБА

Kak grom sr'edí yásnovo n'éba

Like a thunder-clap out of a clear sky.

Suddenly, unexpectedly (said of a sudden and suprising event generally of an unpleasant nature).

Cf. Like a bolt from the blue/out of a clear sky.

200. КАК ДВАЖДЫ ДВА ЧЕТЫРЕ

kak dvázhdy dva chetýr'e

Like two times two is four.

$$2 \times 2 = 4$$

Easy to see or comprehend; as plain or clear as can be; obvious to everyone.

Cf. As plain as a pikestaff; as plain as the nose on your face. 127

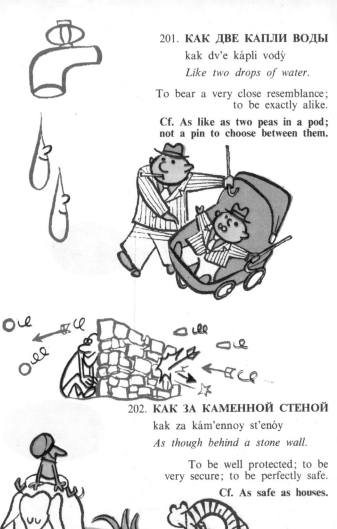

201. КАК ДВЕ КАПЛИ ВОДЫ

kak dv'e kápli vodý

Like two drops of water.

To bear a very close resemblance; to be exactly alike.

Cf. As like as two peas in a pod; not a pin to choose between them.

202. КАК ЗА КАМЕННОЙ СТЕНОЙ

kak za kám'ennoy st'enóy

As though behind a stone wall.

To be well protected; to be very secure; to be perfectly safe.

Cf. As safe as houses.

203. КАК ИЗ-ПОД ЗЕМЛИ ВЫРОС

kak is-pod z'emlí výros

As if grown up from under the ground.

Someone appeared all of a sudden, unexpectedly, from nowhere.

Cf. Out of the blue.

204. КАК ИЗ РОГА ИЗОБИЛИЯ

kak iz róga izobíliya

As if out of the horn of plenty.

In great plenty, in abundance.

205. КАК КОРОВА ЯЗЫКОМ СЛИЗАЛА

kak koróva yazykóm slizála

As if a cow has licked it off with its tongue.

Someone or something has disappeared without a trace.

Cf. To vanish/disappear into thin air.

206. КАК НА ИГОЛКАХ

kak na igólkakh

As if on needles.

Racked with anxiety, in a
state of acute discomfort,
uneasiness or suspense.

**Cf. To be on tenter-hooks;
to be on pins and needles;
to be on thorns/wires.**

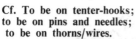

207. КАК НЕБО ОТ ЗЕМЛИ

kak n'ébo ot z'emlí

As far off as heaven from earth.

To differ essentially, sharply, strongly.

Cf. There is a world of difference between them.

208. КАК ОБ СТЕНКУ ГОРОХ

kak ob st'énku gorókh

Like throwing peas against the wall.

To say something to which not the slightest attention is paid (often uttered in irritation.)

Cf. You might as well talk to a brick wall/to the wind.

131

209. КАК ПО МАСЛУ

kak po máslu

Like sliding on oil.

Things are going well, smoothly, swimmingly, without any obstruction or complication.

Cf. Like clockwork; without a hitch.

210. КАК ПО НОТАМ РАЗЫГРАТЬ

kak po nótam razygrát'

As if played from music.

To accomplish something without any difficulty, efficiently, according to a carefully thought-out plan; to perform something with clockwork precision.

211. КАК РУКОЙ СНЯЛО

kak rukóy sn'álo

As if taken off by the hand.

Suddenly gone, completely disappeared as if by magic (usually said of pain or fatigue).

212. КАК РЫБА В ВОДЕ

kak rýba v vod'é

Like a fish in water.

To feel free and easy; to be in suitable or satisfying surroundings; to find something natural and easy to do.

Cf. To feel in one's element; to feel quite at home; to take to something like a duck to water.

133

213. КАК С ГУСЯ ВОДА

kak s gús'a vodá

Like water off a goose.

Without producing any effect;
without paying the slightest attention.

Cf. Like water off a duck's back.

214. КАК СЕЛЬДЕЙ В БОЧКЕ

kak sel'd'éy v bóchk'e

Like herrings in a barrel.

The place is so crowded that
one can't push one's way through.

Cf. Packed like sardines.

215. КАК СКВОЗЬ ЗЕМЛЮ ПРОВАЛИЛСЯ

kak skvoz' z'éml'u provalils'a

As if someone or something has fallen through the ground.

Someone or something has suddenly and unexpectedly disappeared in a mysterious manner, without a trace.

Cf. To vanish into thin air; as though the earth had opened and swallowed it up.

216. КАК СНЕГ НА ГОЛОВУ

kak sn'eg ná golovu

Like snow onto the head.

To appear or arrive suddenly and unexpectedly.

Cf. To come like a bolt from/out of the blue; to drop from the clouds.

217. КАК ЧЁРТ ОТ ЛАДАНА

kak chort ot ládana

Like the devil running away from the incense.

To get rid of or shun someone or something.

Cf. To avoid someone or something like the plague.

218. КАМЕНЬ НА СЕРДЦЕ

kám'en' na s'értse

A stone on one's heart.

Someone feels depressed or unhappy.

Cf. A heavy heart; to have something weigh upon one's heart.

219. КАМЕНЬ С ДУШИ СВАЛИЛСЯ

kám'en' s dushý svalils'a

A stone has fallen off one's heart.

Someone feels relieved of a burden of an upleasant, sad or oppressive feeling.

Cf. A load off one's mind.

220. КАМНЯ НА КАМНЕ НЕ ОСТАВИТЬ

kámn'a na kámn'e n'e ostávit'

Not to leave one stone upon another stone.

To criticize something severely by pointing out the weak points or faults; to utterly demolish an argument.

**Cf. To pull/take something to pieces;
to make mincemeat of something.**

221. КАПЛЯ В МОРЕ

kápl'a v mór'e

A drop in the sea.

A part so small as to be insignificant.

Cf. A drop in the ocean/bucket.

222. КАТАТЬСЯ КАК СЫР В МАСЛЕ

katáttsa kak syr v másl'e

To be rolling like cheese in butter.

To be comfortably off.

Cf. To live in clover; to live on the fat of the land; to live like a king.

223. КАТИТЬСЯ ПОД ГОРУ

katítsa pód goru

To slide downhill.

To deteriorate, to decline, to become worse.

Cf. To go downhill.

224. КАШИ НЕ СВАРИШЬ с кем-либо

káshy n'e svárish

You won't cook kasha* with someone.

You can't get on with someone;
you won't get anywhere with someone;
it's defficult to work with someone.

---

*kasha–a dish of cooked
grain or groats.

139

255. КИДАЕТ В ЖАР

kidáyet v zhar

Thrown into a heat.

He/she becomes extremely agitated or anxious; he/she feels hot all over.

226. КЛЕВАТЬ НОСОМ

kl'evát' nósom

To peck with one's nose.

To nod; to be drowsy.

227. КЛИН КЛИНОМ ВЫШИБАТЬ

klin klínom vyshybát'
To drive out one wedge with another.

To destroy the results of an action by the means this action has been previously caused.

**Cf. To fight fire with fire;
like cures like; nail drives out nail.**

228. КОГДА РАК СВИСТНЕТ

kogdá rak svísn'et
When the crayfish whistles.

No one knows when; never.
**Cf. When pigs fly; when two
Fridays come together.**

229. КОТ НАПЛАКАЛ

kot naplákal

Something the cat cried out.

Very little; practically nothing;
nothing to speak of.

230. КОШКИ СКРЕБУТ НА ДУШЕ

kóshki skr'ebút na dushé

Cast are scratching on one's soul.

To be melancholy, sad, depressed;
to be anxious about something.

Cf. To be sick at heart; to have the blues.

231. КРАЕУГОЛЬНЫЙ КАМЕНЬ

krayeugól'ny kám'en'

A corner-stone.

Something indispensable, essential, of primary importance; a fundamental idea.

Cf. A corner-stone.

232. КРАСИВЫЙ ЖЕСТ

krasívy zhest

A fine gesture.

A deliberate action intended for effect.

Cf. A fine gesture; beau geste.

233. КРАСНЫЙ КАК РАК

krásny kak rak

Red as a lobster.

Red-faced; flushed with anger or embarrassment.

Cf. Red as a lobster.

234. КРЕПКИЙ ОРЕШЕК

kr'épky or'éshek

A hard nut.

A problem that is very hard to solve; a person hard to deal with.

Cf. A hard nut to crack.

235. **КРИЧАТЬ** о чём-либо **НА ВСЕХ ПЕРЕКРЁСТКАХ**

krichát' na vs'ekh p'er'ekr'óstkakh

To shout about something at all cross-roads.

To announce something in the most public manner possible:
to make something generally known to a wide public;
to talk constantly about something.

**Cf. To cry/shout from
the house-tops.**

236. **КРОВЬ С МОЛОКОМ**

krov' s molokóm

Blood with milk.

Someone with fresh complexion,
in the best of health;
one who looks quite well.

Cf. The very picture of health.

237. КТО В ЛЕС, КТО ПО ДРОВА

kto v l'es kto po drová

Some to the forest, some to gather firewood.

A phrase expressing lack of coordination or harmony (often said of singing or playing musical instruments).

238. КУДА ВЕТЕР ДУЕТ

kudá v'ét'er dúyet

Whither the wind is blowing.

One has no firm convictions; one adapts himself to the prevailing opinions, views, tastes; one avoids taking action or making a decision until he sees which move will be most favourable to himself.

Cf. To see/find out which way the wind blows; to see which way the cat jumps; as changeable as a weathercock.

239. КУПИТЬ КОТА В МЕШКЕ
kupít' kotá v m'eshk'é
To buy a cat in a sack.

To buy a thing without knowing its
real value or quality.

Cf. To buy a pig in a poke.

240. КУРАМ НА СМЕХ
kúram ná sm'ekh
For the hens to laugh at.

It's funny, ridiculous, absurd, silly.

Cf. It's enough to make a cat laugh. 147

241. КУСАТЬ СЕБЕ ЛОКТИ

kusát' s'eb'é lókti

To bite one's own elbows.

To be deeply vexed; to be upset over an irreparable loss of someone or something.

Cf. To cry over spilt milk; to kick oneself over a lost opportunity.

242—257

242. ЛЁГКАЯ РУКА

l'ókhkaya ruká

A light hand.
Someone is known
to bring luck to any
kind of undertaking.

243. ЛЁГОК НА ПОДЪЁМ

l'ógok na pod'yóm

Easy on the ascent.

Always ready and willing to go somewhere or do something.

Cf. Quick off the mark; quick on one's toes.

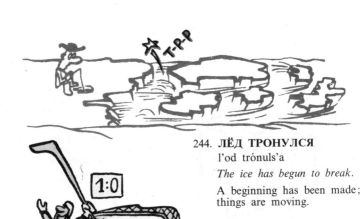

244. ЛЁД ТРОНУЛСЯ

l'od trónuls'a

The ice has begun to break.

A beginning has been made; things are moving.

245. ЛЕЗТЬ В БУТЫЛКУ

l'ezt' v butýlku

To climb into the bottle.

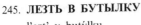

To be carried away by excitement, to lose self-control,
to become suddenly or violently angry (usually
without reason, over a mere trifle).

Cf. To fly off the handle; to blow one's top.

246. ЛЕЗТЬ В ДУШУ

l'ezt' v dúshu

To climb into someone's soul.

To try to find out someone's innermost feellings, thoughts,
intentions; to win someone's favour or confidence.

Cf. To worm oneself into someone's favour/confidence. 151

247. ЛЕЗТЬ ИЗ КОЖИ ВОН

l'ezt' is kózhy von

To climb out of one's skin.

To make a great effort; to do one's utmost, to try one's hardest.

Cf. To lean/bend over backwards; to go out of one's way; to go all out.

248. ЛИТЬ ВОДУ НА чью-либо МЕЛЬНИЦУ

lit' vódu na m'él'nitsu

To pour water on someone's mill-wheel.

Indirectly to help someone (usually an opponent) by one's actions.

Cf. To play into someone's hands; to bring grist to someone's mill.

249. ЛИТЬ КАК ИЗ ВЕДРА

lit' kak iz v'edrá

To pour as from a pail.

To rain heavily.

Cf. It rains cats and dogs.

250. ЛИТЬ КРОКОДИЛОВЫ СЛЁЗЫ

lit' krokodílovy sl'ózy

To shed crocodile tears.

To complain hypocritically; to show insincere, false sorrow.

Cf. To shed crocodile tears. 153

251. ЛОВИТЬ НА ЛЕТУ

lovít' na l'etú

To catch something in flight.

To be quick to comprehend or to learn something; to grasp something easily, at once.

Cf. To be quick on the uptake.

252. ЛОВИТЬ кого-либо НА СЛОВЕ

lovít' na slóv'e

To catch one at one's word.

To make someone do or promise to do what he said he would do.

Cf. To take someone at his word.

253. ЛОВИТЬ РЫБУ В МУТНОЙ ВОДЕ

lovít' rýbu v mútnoy vod'é

To catch fish in turbid water.

To try to benefit from other people's troubles; to try
to gain advantage for oneself from a disturbed state of affairs;
to try to make a calamity by means of personal gain.

Cf. To fish in troubled waters.

254. ЛОМАТЬ ГОЛОВУ над чем-либо

lomát' gólovu

To break one's head over something.

To think hard, especially
on a difficult problem.

**Cf. To rack/cudgel one's
brains over something; to break
one's head over something.**

155

255. ЛОМАТЬ КОПЬЯ

lomát' kóp'ya

To break spears.

To fight for something; to argue heatedly.

Cf. To break a lance with someone over something; to cross swords.

256. ЛОМИТЬСЯ В ОТКРЫТУЮ ДВЕРЬ

lomíttsa v otkrýtuyu dv'er'

To break through an open door.

To assert or try to prove something already well-known and undisputed.

Cf. To force at/knock at an open door.

257. ЛОПНУТЬ КАК МЫЛЬНЫЙ ПУЗЫРЬ

lópnut' kak mýl'ny puzýr'

To burst like a soap-bubble.

Said of something that proves to be unstable, ephemeral or easily destroyed.

ВАВИЛОНСКАЯ БАШНЯ

M

258–273

258. **МАСТЕР НА ВСЕ РУКИ**

mást'er na vs'e rúki

A master at all hands.

To be good at anything one undertakes; to show talent in anything one turns his hand to; a versatile worker.

Cf. A jack-of-all-trades.

259. МАХНУТЬ РУКОЙ

makhnút' rukóy

To wave one's hand at something or someone.

To stop doing something or
dealing with someone; not to care
what happens; to give something
up as a lost or hopeless cause.

260. МЕДВЕДЬ НА УХО НАСТУПИЛ

m'edv'éd' ná ukho nastupíl

A bear stepped on someone's ear.

Someone has no ear for music;
someone is quite tone-deaf.

261. МЕДВЕЖЬЯ УСЛУГА

m'edv'ézh'ya uslúga

A bear's service.

A well-meant action having the opposite effect;
clumsy assistance causing only more problems;
a dubious benefit conferred on someone; a disservice.

262. МЕНЯТЬ КУКУШКУ НА ЯСТРЕБА

m'en'át' kukúshku na yástr'eba

To exchange a cuckoo for a hawk.

To select the worst from among
the worse; to be out of one's
reckoning; to miscalculate.

Cf. To back the wrong horse.

263. МЕРИТЬ НА СВОЙ АРШИН

m'érit' na svoy arshýn

To measure by one's own arshin.*

To judge others by oneself; to apply one's own standard to others.

Cf. To measure another's corn by one's own bushel.

---

* arshin – a ruler one arshin
in length equivalent
to 28 inches.

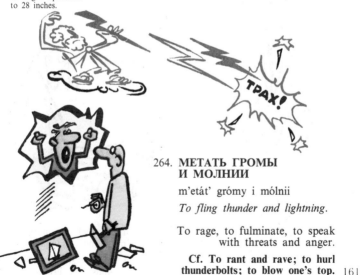

264. МЕТАТЬ ГРОМЫ И МОЛНИИ

m'etát' grómy i mólnii

To fling thunder and lightning.

To rage, to fulminate, to speak
with threats and anger.

**Cf. To rant and rave; to hurl
thunderbolts; to blow one's top.** 161

265. **МИР ТЕСЕН**

mir t'és'en

The world is cramped.

You may unexpectedly run across
a person you know anywhere.

Cf. It's a small world.

266. **МНОГО ВОДЫ УТЕКЛО**

mnógo vodý ut'ekló

Much water has flowed away.

That was long ago; much has happened
since; much has changed since.

**Cf. A lot of water has flowed
under the bridge since.**

162

267. **МОРЕ ПО КОЛЕНО**

mór'e po kol'éno

The sea is knee-deep.

One is unconcerned;
one couldn't care less;
one is absolutely reckless.

Cf. Devil-may-care.

268. **МОТАТЬ СЕБЕ НА УС**

motát' s'eb'é na us

*To wind something
on one's moustache.*

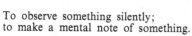

To observe something silently;
to make a mental note of something.

Cf. Bite on that.

163

269. **МОЯ ХАТА С КРАЮ**

moyá kháta s kráyu

My hut is on the periphery.

This has nothing to do with me; its' no business/concern of mine.

270. **МУРАШКИ БЕГАЮТ ПО СПИНЕ**

muráshki b'égayut po spin'é

Little ants run along one's back.

One feels shivery due to fear, horror, or nervous excitement.

**Cf. To give one the creeps; to make one's flesh creep;
to feel chills run up and down one's spine.**

271. МУТИТЬ ВОДУ

mutít' vódu

To muddy the water.

To deliberately muddle matters;
to stir up trouble; to confuse things.

272. МУХИ НЕ ОБИДИТ

múkhi n'e obídit

He/she wouldn't hurt a fly.

He/she is meek, timid, gentle, kind.

**Cf. He wouldn't hurt/harm a fly;
he won't say "boo" to a goose.**

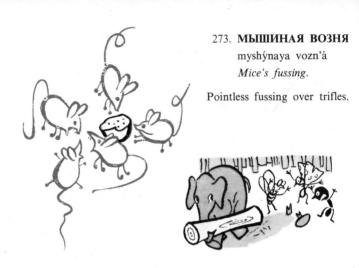

273. **МЫШИНАЯ ВОЗНЯ**
myshýnaya vozn'á
Mice's fussing.

Pointless fussing over trifles.

H

274–325

274. **НАБИТЬ РУКУ**

nabít' rúku

To strengthen one's hand.

To practise so as to acquire skill, to develop a good
technique in something; to become a practised
hand at something; to give oneself a steady hand.

Cf. To get the knack of something. 167

275. НАБРАТЬ В РОТ ВОДЫ

nabrát' v rot vodý

To fill one's mouth with water.

To remain silent; not to utter a word.

Cf. To keep mum.

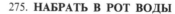

276. НА ВЕС ЗОЛОТА

na v'es zólota

Worth its weight in gold.

Someone or something is extremely
valuable or useful.

Cf. To be worth one's/its weight in gold.

277. НАВОСТРИТЬ ЛЫЖИ

navostrít' lýzhy

To sharpen the skis.

To flee, to run away.

**Cf. To take to one's heels;
to show a clean pair of heels.**

278. НАВОСТРИТЬ УШИ

navostrít' úshy

To sharpen one's ears.

To give sudden and intense attention to what
is being said or to what is going to be said.

Cf. To prick up one's ears.

279. НАВЯЗНУТЬ В ЗУБАХ

nav'áznut' v zubákh

To get stuck in one's teeth.

To have had more than enough;
to be sick and tired of something.

Cf. To set one's teeth on edge.

280. НАДЕЯТЬСЯ КАК НА КАМЕННУЮ ГОРУ

nad'éyattsa kak na kám'ennuyu góru

To rely on someone as on a rock mountain.

To rely fully on someone or something.

281. НАДУТЬ ГУБЫ

nadút' gúby

To blow up one's lips.

To be angry, to take offence wearing a sulky expression;
to express dissatisfaction or displeasure;
to be in a disagreeable mood.

Cf. To pout.

282. НАЖИМАТЬ НА ВСЕ КНОПКИ

nazhimát' na vs'e knópki

To press on all the buttons.

To use every direct or indirect means in order
to attain a goal; to exert personal and private influence
on a matter affecting oneself or others.

Cf. To pull wires/strings. 171

283. НАЖИМАТЬ НА ВСЕ ПЕДАЛИ

nazhimát' na vs'e p'edáli

To press all the pedals.

To do everything in one's power to carry out a task, a promise, etc.

Cf. To go all out.

284. НАЗЫВАТЬ ВЕЩИ СВОИМИ ИМЕНАМИ

nazyvát' v'éshchy svoími im'enámi

To call things by their names.

To speak frankly, plainly or bluntly.

Cf. To call things by their right/proper names; to call a spade a spade.

285. **НАЙТИ СЕБЯ**

naytí s'eb'á

To find oneself.

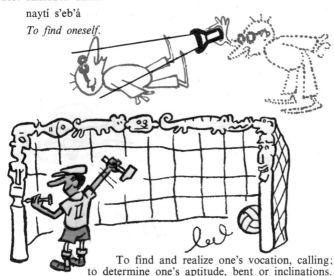

To find and realize one's vocation, calling;
to determine one's aptitude, bent or inclinations.

286. **НАКЛЕИВАТЬ ЯРЛЫКИ**

nakl'éivat' yarlykí

To stick labels on someone or something.

To give a standard or stereotyped estimation
of someone or something (usually of a negative nature).

Cf. To pin a label on someone. 173

287. НА ЛБУ НАПИСАНО

na lbu napísano

It's written on the forehead.

Something about a person is quite obvious by the look on his face.

Cf. It's written all over his face.

288. НАЛОМАТЬ ДРОВ

nalomát' drov

To break up some firewood.

To commit follies; to make a mess of things.

289. НАМЫЛИТЬ ШЕЮ

namýlit' shéyu

To soap someone's neck.

To reprimand or criticize someone sharply; to give someone a good rating.

Cf. To haul someone over the coals; to give someone a dressing-down.

290. НАНЕСТИ УДАР ИЗ-ЗА УГЛА

nan'esti udár iz-za uglá

To strike a blow from round the corner.

To act in an underhand, treacherous, sly manner.

Cf. A stab in the back.

291. НАПУСТИТЬ ТУМАНУ

napustít' tumánu

To let the fog in.

To obscure the issue;
to befog something;
to confuse things;
to try to mislead someone.

292. НАСОЛИТЬ кому-либо

nasolít'

To salt someone.

To spite; to cause someone
annoyance; to do someone
a bad turn.

293. **НАСТУПАТЬ** кому-либо **НА ПЯТКИ**

nastupát' na p'átki

To step on someone's heels.

To catch up with someone; to follow
someone very closely; to be close behind.

Cf. To be at someone's heels.

294. **НАХОДИТЬСЯ НА ТОЧКЕ ЗАМЕРЗАНИЯ**

nakhodíttsa na tóchk'e zam'erzániya

To be at freezing-point.

To remain in the same state or condition without
developing or progressing; to be at a standstill.

295. НАШЛА КОСА НА КАМЕНЬ

nashlá kosá na kám'en'

The scythe has struck a stone.

A clash of conflicting personalities, interests, opinions, etc.

Cf. One has met his match; diamond cut diamond.

296. НЕ ВИДАТЬ КАК СВОИХ УШЕЙ

n'e vidát' kak svoíkh ushéy

One won't see it as his own ears.

One will never see, get or possess something or someone.

Cf. You won't see hide nor hair of something or someone; you have to kiss it good-bye.

297. НЕ ВИДЕТЬ ДАЛЬШЕ СВОЕГО НОСА

n'e víd'et' dal'she svoyevó nósa

Not to see farther than one's nose.

To lack imagination or insight; to be conscious only of circumstances round one; the situation one is now in or events that are presently happening.

Cf. Not to see an inch beyond one's nose; to see no further than one's nose.

298. НЕ ВИДЕТЬ ЛЕСА ЗА ДЕРЕВЬЯМИ

n'e vid'et' l'ésa za d'er'év'yami

Not to see the wood beyond the trees.

To be unable to get a clear view of the whole because of too many details.

Cf. To be unable to see the forest/wood for the trees. 179

299. НЕ ВИДЕТЬ СВЕТА БЕЛОГО

n'e víd'et' sv'éta b'élovo

Not to see the white world.

One is so burdened with work or
cares that he has no peace,
no rest and can't lead a normal life.

300. НЕ ВЫХОДИТ ИЗ ГОЛОВЫ

n'e vykhódit iz golový

It doesn't come out of one's head.

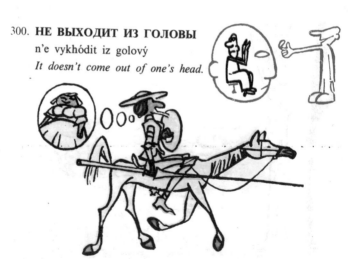

Something remains permanently in one's mind;
one is unable to get something out of one's mind.

180 Cf. **It sticks in one's mind.**

301. **НЕ ЗА ГОРАМИ**
n'e za gorámi
Not beyond the hills.

Something is about
to happen very soon.
Cf. Near at hand.

302. **НЕ ЛЕЗТЬ ЗА СЛОВОМ В КАРМАН**
n'e l'ezt' za slóvom v karmán
Not to climb for a word into one's pocket.

To be quick to respond, to answer promptly
and well; not to be at a loss for words.

Cf. To have a ready/quick tongue. 181

303. НЕМ КАК РЫБА

n'em kak rýba

Dumb as a fish.

Someone says very little or nothing; reserved, uncommunicative.

Cf. Close/dumb as an oyster; silent as a grave; tight-lipped.

304. НЕ МЫТЬЁМ, ТАК КАТАНЬЕМ

n'e myt'yóm tak kátan'yem

If not by washing, then by mangling.

To try to get something; to annoy or vex someone by any means, right or wrong.

Cf. By hook or by crook.

305. НЕ НАХОДИТЬ СЕБЕ МЕСТА

n'e nakhodít' s'eb'é m'ésta

To be unable to find a place for oneself.

To be extremely anxious, discontented; to fret, to worry; not to know what to do with oneself.

306. НЕ НЮХАТЬ ПОРОХУ

n'e n'úkhat' pórokhu

Not to smell gun-powder.

Not to have been in combat.

307. НЕ ОТ МИРА СЕГО

n'e ot míra s'evó

Not of this world.

A person whose mind is filled with visionary thoughts;
one who is too imaginative instead of attending to things
in a practical way; a day-dreamer.

Cf. To be in another world; to have one's head in the clouds.

308. НЕ УДАРИТЬ В ГРЯЗЬ ЛИЦОМ

n'e udárit' v gr'az' litsóm

Not to strike the mud with one's face.

To maintain one's dignity; to acquit oneself well;
not to disgrace oneself; to try to appear at one's best.

Cf. To put one's best foot forward; to make a good showing.

309. НЕ УМЕТЬ ДВУХ СЛОВ СВЯЗАТЬ

n'e um'ét' dvukh slov sv'azát'

To be unable to tie two words together.

To be unable to formulate
one's ideas or express
one's thoughts; to be incoherent.

Cf. He can't put two words together.

310. НЕ ФУНТ ИЗЮМУ

n'e funt iz'úmu

That's not a pound of raisins.

It's not a trifle; it's not
to be regarded as negligible
or unimportant; it's no
light matter; it's no joke.

Cf. It's not to be sneezed/sniffed at. 185

311. НЕЧИСТ НА РУКУ

n'echíst ná ruku

Having an uncleam hand.

Inclined to stealing, swindling or cheating; dishonest, underhanded.
Cf. To be light-fingered.

312. НЕ ЧУЯТЬ НОГ ПОД СОБОЙ

n'e chúyat' nog pod sobóy

Not to feel one's feet under oneself.

To be very happy, to be highly delighted.
**Cf. To be beside oneself with joy;
to tread/walk on air.**

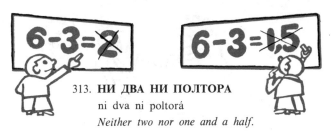

313. НИ ДВА НИ ПОЛТОРА

ni dva ni poltorá

Neither two nor one and a half.

Defies classification; neither good not bad;
neither one thing nor the other.

314. НИ ЖИВ НИ МЁРТВ

ni zhiv ni m'ortv

Neither alive nor dead.

Despondent; petrified with fear or astonishment.

Cf. More dead than alive.

315. НИ ЗА КАКИЕ КОВРИЖКИ
ni za kakíye kovrízhki
Not for any gingerbread.

Not for anything; not on any account.
Cf. Not for the world; not on your life.

316. НИ КОЛА НИ ДВОРА
ni kolá ni dvorá
Neither a picket nor a yard.

To be very poor; not to have a roof over one's head.

Cf. To have neither house nor home.

317. НИ К СЕЛУ НИ К ГОРОДУ

ni k s'elú ni k górodu

Neither to the village nor to the town.

Beside the point, out of place; for no apparent reason; quite irrelevantly

Cf. Neither here nor there.

318. НИ НА ЧТО НЕ ПОХОЖЕ

ni na shto n'e pokhózhe

It doesn't look like anything.

Very bad; unthinkable; unheard of; like nothing on earth; that won't do; that's no good at all.

319. НИ ПУХА НИ ПЕРА!

ni púkha ni p'erá
Neither down nor feather.

Good luck!

320. НИ РЫБА НИ МЯСО

ni rýba ni m'áso
Neither fish nor meat.

A mediocre person.

Cf. Neither fish, flesh nor fowl.

321. НОЖ ОСТРЫЙ
nozh óstry
A sharp knife.

Something extremely unpleasant or painful;
something is the source of annoyance, grief, etc.

Cf. Gall and wormwood; this is sheer agony/hell.

322. НОМЕР НЕ ПРОЙДЁТ
nóm'er n'e proyd'ót
The number won't pass through.

That won't do; you can't get away with it.

**Cf. Nothing doing; that trick
won't work; that won't wash.**

191

323. НОСА НЕ ВЫСУНУТЬ

nósa n'e výsunut'

Not to peep out one's nose.

One can't go outside.

Cf. One can't even stick his nose out of the house.

324. НОСИТЬ ВОДУ РЕШЕТОМ

nosít' vódu r'eshetóm

To carry water in a sieve.

To do something useless;
to waste time.

Cf. To plough the sand.

325. НУЖЕН КАК ПРОШЛОГОДНИЙ СНЕГ

núzhen kak proshlogódny sn'eg

As needed as last year's snow.

There is no need to.

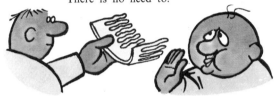

326–346

326. **ОБВЕСТИ ВОКРУГ ПАЛЬЦА**
obv'estí vokrúg pál'tsa
To lead someone round a finger.

Without any difficulty
to make a person do exactly
what one wishes; to be able
to handle or manage someone
with ease; to cajole,
persuade someone artfully.

**Cf. To twist/turn someone
round one's little finger.**

327. ОБЕЩАТЬ ЗОЛОТЫЕ ГОРЫ

ob'eshchát' zolotýye góry

To promise mountains of gold.

To promise someone a fortune; to make extravagant promises.

Cf. To promise the moon.

328. ОБИВАТЬ ПОРОГИ

obivát' porógi

To knock against the thresholds.

To go frequently somewhere trying to obtain something; to apply or petition with dogged persistence.

Cf. To haund someone's threshold; to camp on someone's doorstep.   195

329. ОБРАТИТЬСЯ НЕ ПО АДРЕСУ

obratíttsa n'e po ádr'esu
To apply to the wrong address.

To come to the wrong person or place to get what one requires.

Cf. To come to the wrong shop.

330. ОДИН КАК ПЕРСТ

odín kak p'erst
Alone as a finger.

All alone in the world; all by oneself; without kinfolk.

331. ОДНА НОГА ЗДЕСЬ, ДРУГАЯ ТАМ

odná nogá zd'es' drugáya tam
One foot's here, the other's there.

To go and fetch, to run and fetch;
to do something very quickly, with lightning speed.

332. ОДНОГО ПОЛЯ ЯГОДА

odnovó pól'a yágoda
A berry from the same field.

They look alike; they are similar in disposition,
tastes, etc.; they are well matched; they deserve
each other; one is no better than the other.

**Cf. Not a pin to choose between them; cut from
the same cloth; birds of one feather.**

197

333. ОКАЗАТЬСЯ МЕЖДУ ДВУХ ОГНЕЙ

okazáttsa m'ézhdu dvukh ogn'éy

To find oneself between two fires.

To be or find oneself between two
equally serious evils or dangers,
between equally unpleasant alternatives, in a perplexing situation;
to be attacked from two directions; to be criticized from both sides.

Cf. Between the devil and the deep blue sea; between two fires.

334. ОКАЗАТЬСЯ МЕЖДУ НЕБОМ И ЗЕМЛЁЙ

okazáttsa m'ézhdu n'ébom i z'eml'óy

To find oneself between the sky and the earth.

To be homeless; not to have
a roof over one's head.

335. ОКАТИТЬ ХОЛОДНОЙ ВОДОЙ

okatít' kholódnoy vodóy

To pour cold water over someone.

To disparage someone, to discourage someone's enthusiasm; to damp someone's ardour; to throw someone into confusion.

Cf. To throw/pour cold water on/over someone.

336. ОКУНУТЬСЯ С ГОЛОВОЙ

okunúttsa z golovóy

To plunge headlong.

To become utterly absorbed/engrossed in something; to be deeply immersed, irrevocably involved.

Cf. To be up to one's ears in something; to throw oneself into something.

199

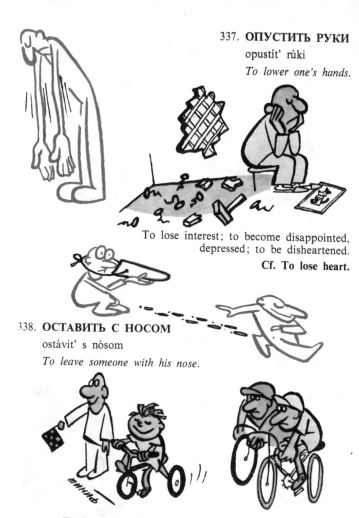

337. ОПУСТИТЬ РУКИ

opustít' rúki

To lower one's hands.

To lose interest; to become disappointed, depressed; to be disheartened.

Cf. To lose heart.

338. ОСТАВИТЬ С НОСОМ

ostávit' s nósom

To leave someone with his nose.

To leave someone without something he had hoped for; to make a fool of someone; to trick someone.

Cf. To leave someone holding the bag.

339. ОСТАТЬСЯ НА БОБАХ

ostáttsa na bobákh

To be left on the beans.

To be left without something one has hoped for; to be out in one's reckoning; to get nothing for one's pains; to be left with nothing.

Cf. To be left holding the bag.

340. ОСТАТЬСЯ У РАЗБИТОГО КОРЫТА

ostáttsa u razbítovo korýta

To be left at the broken wash-tub.

To be left with nothing, having lost everything one had; to be no better off than when one started.

Cf. To be back at the bottom of the ladder.

341. ОТКЛАДЫВАТЬ НА ЧЁРНЫЙ ДЕНЬ

otkládyvat' na chórny d'en'

To put aside for a black day.

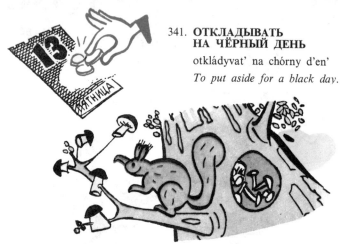

To save or reserve something (usually one's income)
for time of trouble, for bad times.

Cf. To save/put by for a rainy day.

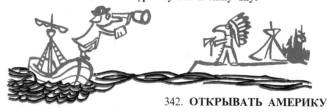

342. ОТКРЫВАТЬ АМЕРИКУ

otkryvát' am'ériku

To discover America.

To say something that everyone has long been aware of;
to say or explain something that is already well known
to everyone; to retail stale news.

Cf. The Dutch have taken Holland; Queen Anne is dead!

343. **ОТКРЫВАТЬ** кому-либо **ГЛАЗА**
на кого-либо / что-либо

otkryvát' glazá

To open someone's eyes to someone or something.

To enable one to understand, to cause to be aware of or to realise a fact, truth, reality to which one had been blind.

Cf. To open someone's eyes to something or someone.

344. **ОТКРЫВАТЬ** кому-либо **ДУШУ/СЕРДЦЕ**

otkryvát' dúshu/s'értse

To open one's soul/heart to someone.

To tell someone frankly of one's innermost thoughts or feelings.

Cf. To lay bare one's heart.

203

345. ОТКРЫВАТЬ СВОИ КАРТЫ

otkryvát' svoyí kárty

To show one's cards.

To stop making secrets of one's plans or intentions; to reveal candidly all one's aims.

Cf. To lay/put one's cards on the table; to show one's hand.

346. ОТКУДА СЫР-БОР ЗАГОРЕЛСЯ

otkúda syr-bor zagor'éls'a

That's how the wet pine forest caught fire.

That's how it all started (usually about something unpleasant or troublesome).

Cf. That was the spark that set the forest on fire.

204

П

347–436

347. ПАЛЕЦ О ПАЛЕЦ НЕ УДАРИТЬ

pál'ets o pál'ets n'e udárit'

Not to strike one finger against another.

To be idle; not to stir oneself; not to make the slightest effort to attain one's goal.

Cf. Not to raise/lift a finger.

348. ПАЛКА О ДВУХ КОНЦАХ

pálka o dvukh kontsákh

A staff with two ends.

Something that can have pleasant and unpleasant consequences; something that can bring good as well as harm.

Cf. A double-edged/two-edged weapon; it cuts both ways.

349. ПАЛЬЦА В РОТ НЕ КЛАДИ

pál'tsa v rot n'e kladí

Don't put your finger in his/her mouth.

Someone is not to be trifled with; with this man one must be scrupulously

exact; one must be on one's guard with him because he is likely to take advantage of another's false step.

350. **ПАЛЬЦЕМ** кого-либо **НЕ ТРОНУТЬ**

pál'tsem n'e trónut'

Not to touch anyone with one's finger.

Not to do anyone any harm; not to hit someone.

Cf. Not to hurt a fly.

351. **ПАЛЬЧИКИ ОБЛИЖЕШЬ**

pál'chiki oblízhesh

You'll lick your fingers clean.

Delicious, tasty, appetising food or drink; a real treat.

Cf. Finger-licking good.

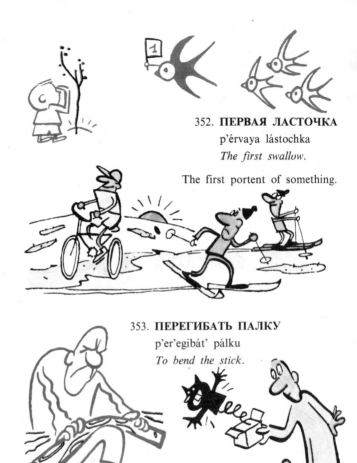

352. ПЕРВАЯ ЛАСТОЧКА
p'érvaya lástochka
The first swallow.

The first portent of something.

353. ПЕРЕГИБАТЬ ПАЛКУ
p'er'egibát' pálku
To bend the stick.

To go beyond the appointed or accepted limit;
to go to the extreme; to go too far; to overdo something.

208 **Cf. To overshoot the mark.**

354. ПЕРЕЛИВАТЬ ИЗ ПУСТОГО В ПОРОЖНЕЕ

p'er'elivát' is pustóvo v porózhn'eye

To pour something from one empty vessel into another.

To waste time on something useless;
to waste time in useless debate; to engage in idle chatter.

Cf. To mill the wind; to beat the air.

355. ПЕРЕЛОМИТЬ СЕБЯ

p'er'elomít' seb'á

To break oneself in two.

To master oneself; to conquer one's temper; to change one's
behaviour, character, habits; to restrain or suppress one's
feelings; to overcome oneself or something in oneself. 209

356. ПЕРЕМЫВАТЬ КОСТОЧКИ

p'er'emyvát' kóstochki

To wash someone's bones.

To gossip, to say spiteful things about someone;
to find detailed faults in a person.

Cf. To pick/pull someone to pieces.

357. ПЕРЕПОЛНИТЬ ЧАШУ ТЕРПЕНИЯ

p'er'epólnit' cháshu t'erp'éniya

To overfill the cup of patience.

To bring someone to the end of his endurance or patience;
to exasperate someone; to be at the end of one's tether.

210 **Cf. The last straw; to break the camel's back.**

358. **ПЕСЕНКА СПЕТА**

p'és'enka sp'éta

One's song has been sung.

One is near his end; one is ruined; it's all done with him; he's done for.

Cf. Someone's goose is cooked.

359. **ПИСАТЬ КАК КУРИЦА ЛАПОЙ**

pisát' kak kúritsa lápoy

To write like a chicken with its claw.

To write quite indecipherably.

Cf. One's handwriting is like chicken tracks.

360. ПЛАВАТЬ КАК ТОПОР

plávat' kak topór

To swim like an axe.

To be a poor swimmer or not to be able to swim at all.

Cf. To swim like a stone/like a tailor's goose.

361. ПЛАКАТЬСЯ В ЖИЛЕТКУ

plákattsa v zhil'étku

To weep into someone's waistcoat.

To bewail one's fate seeking sympathy or consolation.

Cf. To cry on someone's shoulder.

362. ПЛАТИТЬ ТОЙ ЖЕ МОНЕТОЙ

platít' toy zhe mon'étoy

To pay someone back in the same coin.

To act by using on an opponent the same methods he employed against one; to return like for like; to retaliate.

Cf. To pay one back in his own coin; to pay/answer back in kind.

363. ПЛЕВАТЬ В ПОТОЛОК

pl'evát' v potolók

To spit at the ceiling.

To do nothing at all; to be idle.

Cf. To fritter away the time; to sit twiddling one's thumbs.

213

364. ПЛЕСТИСЬ КАК ЧЕРЕПАХА

pl'estís' kak cher'epákha

To crawl like a tortoise.

To go very slowly;
to drag oneself along; to trudge.

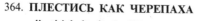

Cf. To go at a crawl; to move at a snail's pace.

365. ПЛЫТЬ ПО ТЕЧЕНИЮ

plyt' po t'echéniyu

To go down stream.

To do or think as most people do; to allow one's actions
and principles to be guided solely by the prevailing trend;
to be carried away by the course of events.

Cf. To go/swim with the stream/current; to follow the crowd.

366. **ПОБЫВАТЬ В** чьей-либо **ШКУРЕ**

pobyvát' v shkúr'e

To be in someone else's hide.

To be in the same unpleasant position
or adverse circumstances as someone else.

Cf. To be in someone's shoes/skin.

367. **ПОГНАТЬСЯ ЗА ДВУМЯ ЗАЙЦАМИ**

pognáttsa za dvum'á záytsami

To run after two hares.

To persue two different
aims simultaneously.

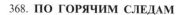

368. ПО ГОРЯЧИМ СЛЕДАМ

po gor'áchim sl'edám

While the tracks are hot.

Without losing time; immediately,
directly after some event.

**Cf. To let no grass grow
under one's feet.**

369. ПОДВЕРНУТЬСЯ ПОД РУКУ

podv'ernúttsa pód ruku

*To turn up under
one's hand.*

Something turns up without one's having
to make a special search for it.

Cf. To come to hand.

370. **ПОДВЕСТИ** кого-либо **ПОД МОНАСТЫРЬ**

podv'estí pod monastýr'

To bring someone up to a monastery.

To put someone into a difficult position; to put someone in a tight spot; to cause someone much trouble.

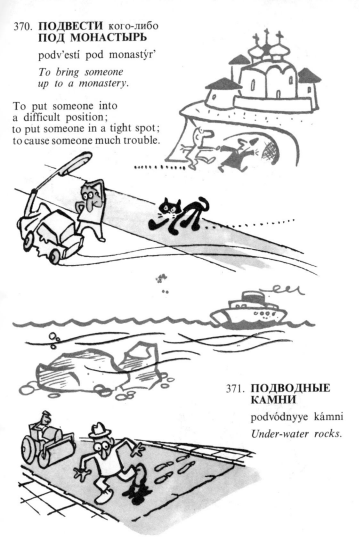

371. **ПОДВОДНЫЕ КАМНИ**

podvódnyye kámni
Under-water rocks.

A difficulty which is hard to foresee; a hidden obstacle; a snag.   217

372. ПОД ГОРЯЧУЮ РУКУ

pod gor'áchuyu rúku

Under a hot hand.

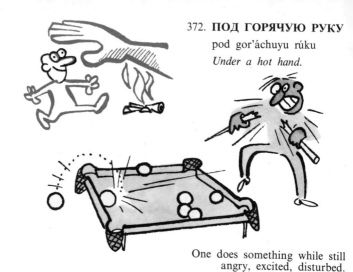

One does something while still angry, excited, disturbed.

Cf. In the heat of the moment.

373. ПОДЖАТЬ ХВОСТ

podzhát' khvost

To turn one's tail between one's legs.

To become more cautious, circumspect;
to cease boasting;
to become less self-assured.

218   **Cf. To have/put one's tail between one's legs; to sing small.**

374. ПОДЛИТЬ МАСЛА В ОГОНЬ

podlít' másla v ogón'

To add oil to the fire.

To act or speak in such a way as to increase the existing passion or excitement; to aggravate the trouble; to make a bad matter worse.

Cf. To add fuel to the fire; to pour oil on the flame.

375. ПОДЛОЖИТЬ СВИНЬЮ

podlozhít' svin'yú

To lay a pig near someone.

To do a vile thing to someone on the sly.

Cf. To play a dirty/mean trick on someone. 219

376. ПОДНЕСТИ ПИЛЮЛЮ

podn'estí pil'úl'u

To bring a pill to someone.

To say or do something unpleasant, annoying, insulting.

Cf. To give someone a bitter pill to swallow.

377. ПОДНИМАТЬ НА ЩИТ

podnimát' na shchit

*To raise something
or someone up
on the shield.*

To extol, to eulogize, to boost.

Cf. To praise to the skies.

378. ПОД НОСОМ
pód nosom
Under one's nose.

Directly in front of one; in plain view; in one's presence.

Cf. Near at hand; under someone's very nose; before someone's face.

379. ПОДНЯТЬ ВСЕХ НА НОГИ
podn'át' vs'ekh ná nogi
To raise everybody to his feet.

To disturb everyone; to raise the alarm; to make everyone be more active; to rouse everyone to action.

221

380. ПОДПИСЫВАТЬСЯ
под чем-либо
ОБЕИМИ РУКАМИ

podpísyvattsa ob'éimi rukámi

To sign something with both hands.

To willingly agree to something;
to fully endorse something.

381. ПОДРЕЗАТЬ
кому-либо **КРЫЛЬЯ**

podr'ézat' krýl'ya

To clip someone's wings.

To limit one's movements, activities; to hamper one's freedom
of action; to destroy one's self-confidence; to undermine
one's power or ability to do something.

222   Cf. To clip/cut someone's wings/claws.

382. **ПОД СУРДИНКУ**

pod surdínku

With a mute.

Softly, gently;
on the quiet;
on the sly;
without being noticed.

383. **ПОЖИНАТЬ ПЛОДЫ**

pozhinát' plodý

To reap the fruits.

To experience the results of
one's actions, deeds, behaviour.

Cf. To reap the fruits of something. 223

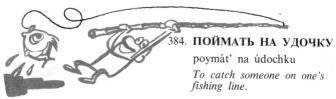

384. ПОЙМАТЬ НА УДОЧКУ

poymát' na údochku

To catch someone on one's fishing line.

By deceiving or outwitting someone to cause him to do something; to trick or to fool someone.

Cf. To catch out.

385. ПОКАЗАТЬ, ГДЕ РАКИ ЗИМУЮТ

pokazát' gd'e ráki zimúyut

To show someone where the crayfish winter.

To teach someone a lesson; to punish someone; to scold someone severely.

Cf. To make it hot for someone; to show someone a thing or two.

386. ПОКАЗАТЬ КОГТИ

pokazát' kógti

To show one's claws.

To show hostility, anger, or resentment;
to display a threatening attitude.

Cf. To show one's teeth.

387. ПОКАЗАТЬ ПЯТКИ

pokazát' p'átki

To show one's heels.

To run away; to escape.

**Cf. To take to one's heels;
to show a clean pair of heels; to take flight.**

388. ПОКАЗА́ТЬ ТОВА́Р ЛИЦО́М

pokázyvat' továr litsóm

To show one's goods fron.

To show a thing from its best side:
to make the best of something;
to show something to its full
advantage;
to display oneself
in a favourable light.

389. ПОЛНАЯ ЧАША

pólnaya chásha

A full cup.

One lives in plenty,
in affluence, in luxury.

390. ПОЛОЖА РУКУ НА СЕРДЦЕ

polozhá rúku ná sertse

With one's hand on one's heart.

To say something quite frankly, candidly, sincerely.

Cf. To say something with one's hand upon one's heart, open-heartedly.

391. ПОЛОЖИТЬ ЗУБЫ НА ПОЛКУ

polozhít' zúby na pólku

To put one's teeth on a shelf.

To go hungry; to starve.

Cf. To tighten one's belt.

392. **ПОЛОЖИТЬ** кого-либо **НА ОБЕ ЛОПАТКИ**

polozhít na ób'e lopátki

To put someone on both his shoulder-blades.

To defeat an opponent in an argument, competition, contest, etc.; to beat someone.

393. **ПОЛОЖИТЬ** что-либо **ПОД СУКНО**

polozhít' pod suknó

To put something under the cloth.

To delay or postpone consideration of an official paper; to pigeon-hole a request or an application; to shelve a problem or a plan.

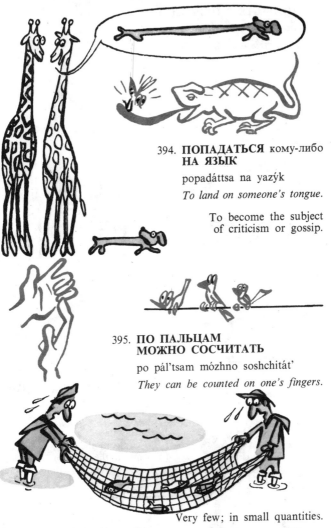

394. ПОПАДАТЬСЯ кому-либо НА ЯЗЫК

popadáttsa na yazýk

To land on someone's tongue.

To become the subject of criticism or gossip.

395. ПО ПАЛЬЦАМ МОЖНО СОСЧИТАТЬ

po pál'tsam mózhno soshchitát'

They can be counted on one's fingers.

Very few; in small quantities.

Cf. You can count them on your fingers. 229

396. ПОПАСТЬ В ПЕРЕПЛЁТ

popást' v per'epl'ót

To get into a binding.

To get into a difficulty or into trouble; to find oneself in an awkward or dangerous situation.

Cf. To get into a scrape/mess/tight corner; to be in a spot; to be/be caught in a bind.

397. ПОПАСТЬ В ТОЧКУ

popást' v tóchku

To hit the right point.

To come to the right conclusion; to come at the crux of the matter; to say or do what is exactly right as if by guessing correctly what must be said or done in the circumstances.

Cf. To hit the nail on the head; to hit the bull's eye/the mark.

398. ПОПАСТЬ КАК КУР ВО ЩИ

popást' kak kur vó shchi

To get oneself into the shchi*
like a chicken.

To get into trouble; to be caught.

Cf. To get/fall into the soup; to get into hot water.

* shchi — cabbage soup

399. ПОПАСТЬ кому-либо
НА ЗУБОК

popást' na zubók

To find oneself on someone's little tooth.

To be subjected to biting or sarcastic
criticism; to become the butt of ridicule.

Cf. To be torn to pieces

400. ПОПАСТЬ НЕ В БРОВЬ, А В ГЛАЗ

popást' n'e v brov' a v glaz

To hit not the eyebrow but the eye.

To guess right; to say something that is exactly right;
to give the true explanation.

Cf. To hit the nail on the head; that hit the mark; you've said it!

401. ПОПАСТЬ ПАЛЬЦЕМ В НЕБО

popást' pál'tsem v n'ébo

To hit the sky with one's finger.

To say or do something that is far from being
correct or quite out of place; to answer
irrelevantly.

**Cf. To get/take the wrong sow by the ear;
to be wide of/way off the mark.**

232

402. ПОПАСТЬСЯ НА чью-либо УДОЧКУ

popásttsa na údochku

To be caught on someone's fishing line.

To permit oneself to be fooled; to fall for a hoax or trap; to accept a proposal, an offer, etc. made to tempt one to do something.

Cf. To swallow the bait; to rise to the fly; to be taken in; to fall into someone's trap/snare.

403. ПОРОХУ НЕ ВЫДУМАЕТ

pórokhu n'e výdumayet

He will not invent gunpowder.

He will never do anything remarkable or outstanding (usually said of a dull-witted, not very bright person).

Cf. He will never set the Thames/world on fire.

404. ПОРОХУ НЕ ХВАТАЕТ

pórokhu n'e khvatáyet

Not enough gunpowder.

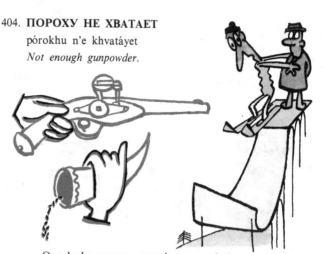

One lacks energy, strenght or resolution to do something.

Cf. It's beyond him; he has not it in him; he is not up to it.

405. ПОСАДИТЬ кого-либо В ГАЛОШУ

posadít' v galóshu

To put someone into a galosh.

To put someone into an embarrasing or uncomfortable situation; to be made fun of; to get someone into a fix; to be in an awkward predicament.

406. ПОСЛЕДНИЙ КРИК МОДЫ

posl'édny krik módy

The latest cry of fashion.

The latest fashion; the latest craze.

Cf. The last word in fashion.

407. ПОСЛЕДНЯЯ КАПЛЯ

posl'édn'aya kápl'a

The last drop.

The final circumstance of a series
that makes a situation
unbearable.

Cf. The last straw. 235

408. ПОСЛЕДНЯЯ СПИЦА В КОЛЕСНИЦЕ

posl'édn'aya spítsa
v kol'esnítse

The last spoke in the chariot.

A person of very little importance;
one who doesn't count; a minor figure.

Cf. A mere cog in the machine.

409. ПОСЛЕ ДОЖДИЧКА В ЧЕТВЕРГ

pósl'e dózhdichka v chetv'érg

After a little rain on a Thursday.

No one knows when.

Cf. When pigs fly; when two Fridays come together.

410. ПОСТАВИТЬ ВОПРОС РЕБРОМ

postávit' voprós r'ebróm

To put a question edgewise.

To announce or state something categorically;
to say something in a manner that leaves no room
for doubt; to ask something directly, openly;
to put a question point-blank

Cf. Not to mince words.

411. ПОСТАВИТЬ ВСЁ НА КАРТУ

postávit' vs'o na kártu

To put everything on the card.

To risk all that one has on a single venture, method, etc.;
to stake all one's hopes on one source or means.

Cf. To put all one's eggs in one basket. 237

412. **ПОСТАВИТЬ** кого-либо **В ТУПИК**

postávit' v tupík

To put someone in a blind alley.

To bewilder, to puzzle, to nonplus someone; to throw someone into confusion.

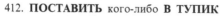

413. **ПОСТАВИТЬ КРЕСТ**
на ком-либо/чём-либо

postávit' kr'est

To put a cross on someone/something.

To lose faith in someone or something; to stop thinking of someone or something; to give someone up for lost; to give something up as a hopeless case.

238 Cf. **To kiss something good-bye.**

414. ПОСТАВИТЬ кого-либо НА СВОЁ МЕСТО

postávit' na svoyó m'ésto

To put someone in his place.

To snub a person who is overstepping his bounds; to check someone's presumption.

Cf. To put someone in his place.

415. ПОЧИВАТЬ НА ЛАВРАХ

pochivát' na lávrakh

To sleep on one's laurels.

To be satisfied with what one has already achieved or accomplished without striving for more.

Cf. To rest on one's laurels.

239

416. **ПРИБИРАТЬ К РУКАМ**

pribirát' k rukám

To take something in one's hands.

To appropriate, to seize, to take possession of.

Cf. To lay one's hands on something.

417. **ПРИВЕСТИ** кого-либо **В СЕБЯ**

priv'estí v s'eb'á

To bring someone into oneself.

To cause someone to
regain consciousness;
to revive someone.

Cf. To bring someone round/to.

418. ПРИЛОЖИТЬ РУКУ
к чему-либо

prilozhít' rúku

To put one's hand to something.

To be actively involved in something (usually reprehensible, blameworthy).

Cf. To have/take a hand in something; to have a finger in the pie.

419. ПРИНИМАТЬ ЗА ЧИСТУЮ МОНЕТУ
prinimát' za chístuyu mon'étu

To take for a pure coin.

To regard something as true; to take something seriously.

Cf. To take in good faith; to take at face value. 241

420. **ПРИПИРАТЬ**
кого-либо **К СТЕНКЕ**

pripirát' k st'énk'e

To press someone against the wall.

To put someone in a difficult or embarrassing position, forcing him to do or admit something; to put someone in desperate straits.

Cf. To drive/push someone to the wall; to drive someone into a corner; to pin someone down.

421. **ПРИТЯНУТЬ** что-либо **ЗА УШИ**

prit'anút' zá ushi

To pull something up by the ears.

To make use of something without adequate grounds; to advance far-fetched arguments.

Cf. To drag something in.

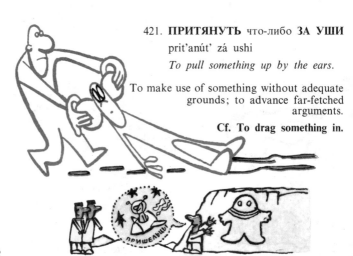

242

422. ПРОБНЫЙ ШАР

próbny shar

A trial ball.

An approach or device (usually by making discreet inquiries) used to clarify a situation or test the opinions or feelings of others.

Cf. A trial balloon; a feeler.

423. ПРОВАЛИТЬСЯ С ТРЕСКОМ

provalíttsa s tr'éskom

To collapse with a bang.

To flop; to be a complete and ignominious failure.

Cf. To come a cropper/crasher; to fall flat on one's face.

424. **ПРОГЛОТИТЬ ПИЛЮЛЮ**

proglotít' pil'úl'u

To swallow the pill.

To disregard an insult; to endure an offence patiently, without resistance or complaint.

Cf. To swallow a bitter pill.

425. **ПРОГЛОТИТЬ ЯЗЫК**

proglotít' yazýk

To swallow one's tongue.

To fall silent; to stop talking.

Cf. To lose one's tongue.

426. ПРОЖУЖЖАТЬ ВСЕ УШИ

prozhuzhzhát' vs'e úshi

To buzz someone's ears through.

To bore someone by telling him something over and over again; to keep dinging something into semeone's ears.

Cf. To talk someone's ears off about something; to drone on at someone; to go rabbiting on.

427. ПРОЙТИ КРАСНОЙ НИТЬЮ

proytí krásnoy nít'yu

To run through something with a red thread.

To be the basic idea, the key-note, the essence of something; to run through something (e.g. a book or a speech).

428. ПРОЙТИ СКВОЗЬ ОГОНЬ И ВОДУ

proytí skvoz' ogón' i vódu

To go through fire and water.

To go through a great deal in life; to encounter or face the greatest dangers or hardest experiences; to endure perils of all kinds.

Cf. To go through fire and water; to go through the mill.

429. ПРОЙТИСЬ ПО чьему-либо АДРЕСУ

proytís' po ádr'esu

To walk up and down someone's address.

To make a snide remark about someone; to make fun of someone; to make an implied criticism.

Cf. To have a fling at someone; to give someone a bad write-up.

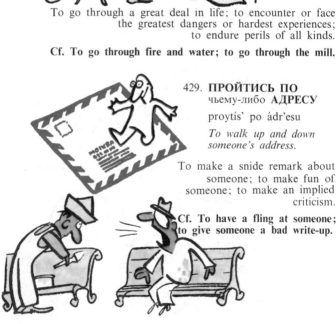

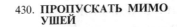

430. ПРОПУСКАТЬ МИМО УШЕЙ

propuskát' mimo ushéy

To let something pass by one's ears.

To pay no attention or not to react to something that has been or is being said.

Cf. To let something go in one ear and out the other.

431. ПРЯТАТЬ КОНЦЫ В ВОДУ

pr'átat' kontsý v vódu

To hide the ends in water.

To destroy evidence; to bury, remove every trace of something; to cover up one's tracks.

Cf. And no one is the wiser.

247

432. ПТИЧЬЕГО МОЛОКА НЕ ХВАТАЕТ

ptích'yevo moloká n'e khvatáyet

Someone lacks bird's milk.

A great abundance of everything.

433. ПУД СОЛИ СЪЕСТЬ
с кем-либо

pud sóli s'yést'

To eat a pood* of salt with someone.

___

* pood — an old Russian unit
of weight (16.38 kg or
approx. 36 1b.).

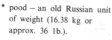

To live with or know someone for a long time;
to spend a long time together with someone.

434. ПУСКАТЬ КОЗЛА В ОГОРОД

puskát' kozlá v ogoród

To let the goat into the kitchen garden.

To give someone access to a place where he may be particularly harmful or dangerous, or to something from which he wishes to profit.

435. ПУСКАТЬ кому-либо ПЫЛЬ В ГЛАЗА

puskát' pyl' v glazá

To throw dust in someone's eyes.

To make a false impression; to try to impress people with one's superiority, to display oneself; to act in an ostentatious manner.

Cf. To put on airs; to cut a dash; to throw dust in someone's eyes.

436. ПУШКОЙ НЕ ПРОШИБЁШЬ

púshkoy n'e proshib'ósh

You won't breach it with a cannon-ball.

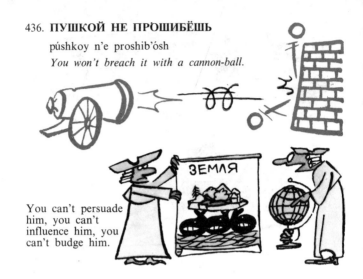

You can't persuade him, you can't influence him, you can't budge him.

P

437–459

437. **РАБОТАТЬ
ЗАСУЧИВ РУКАВА**

rabótat' zasuchív rukavá

To work with one's sleeves rolled up.

To work assiduously, strenuously.

438. РАБОТАТЬ
НЕ ПОКЛАДАЯ РУК

rabótat' n'e pokladáya ruk

To work without giving rest to one's hands.

To work unceasingly, tirelessly, indefatigably.

Cf. To be as busy as a bee.

439. РАЗБИВАТЬСЯ В ЛЕПЁШКУ

razbiváttsa v l'ep'óshku

To smash oneself into a flat cake.

To do one's utmost, to strain every nerve,
to do next to impossible to attain one's end.

Cf. To lay oneself out; to go all out.

440. **РАЗВЕСИТЬ УШИ**

razv'ésit' úshi

To hang out one's ears.

To be so carried away by what one hears that one doesn't react properly or forgets about something important.

441. **РАЗВЯЗАТЬ** кому-либо **РУКИ**

razv'azát' rúki

To untie someone's hands.

To give someone freedom of action, choice or judgement in a matter.

Cf. To give someone a free hand; to untie someone's hands. 253

442. **РАЗВЯЗАТЬ ЯЗЫК**

razv'azát' yazýk

To untie one's tongue.

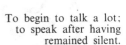

To begin to talk a lot;
to speak after having
remained silent.

**Cf. To loosen one's tongue;
to find one's tongue.**

443. **РАЗРЯДИТЬ АТМОСФЕРУ**

razr'adit' atmosf'éru

To discharge the atmosphere.

To relieve tension; to create
an atmosphere that will cool
down a fiery argument.

Cf. To clear the air.

444. РАСХЛЁБЫВАТЬ КАШУ

raskhl'óbyvat' káshú

*To eat up kasha.**

To disentangle something;
to put things right;
to clear up a mess;
to get oneself out
of a mess.

---

* kasha — a dish of cooked
grain or groats.

445. РВАТЬ И МЕТАТЬ

rvat' i m'etát

To tear and throw.

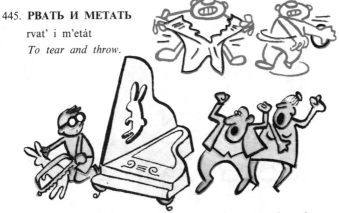

To get irritated; to be in a towering rage; to show angry impatience;
to worry oneself into a state of temper.

Cf. To fret and fume.   255

446. РВАТЬ НА СЕБЕ ВОЛОСЫ

rvat' na s'ebé vólosy

To tear one's hair.

To be desperate; to be distressed; to grieve.

Cf. To tear one's hair.

447. РВАТЬ кого-либо НА ЧАСТИ

rvat' na chásti

To tear someone into pieces.

To pester someone with questions or requests; to bother someone too much; not to give someone any peace.

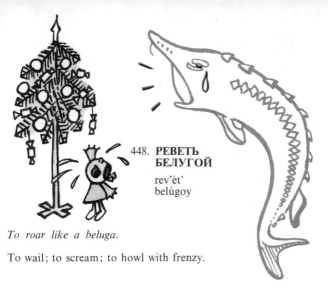

448. **РЕВЕТЬ БЕЛУГОЙ**

rev'ét' belúgoy

To roar like a beluga.

To wail; to scream; to howl with frenzy.

449. **РОДИТЬСЯ В СОРОЧКЕ**

rodíttsa v soróchk'e

To be born with a shirt on.

To be always lucky, successful, happy.

Cf. **To always fall on one's feet; to be born with a silver spoon in one's mouth.** 257

450. РОДИТЬСЯ ПОД СЧАСТЛИВОЙ ЗВЕЗДОЙ

rodittsa pod schaslívoy zv'ezdóy

To be born under a lucky star.

To be always lucky, successful, happy.

**Cf. To always fall on one's feet;
to be born under a lucky star.**

451. РУБИТЬ СПЛЕЧА

rubít' spl'echá

To chop straight from the shoulder.

To speak in a direct, outspoken, blunt way;
without reserve or evasion; to act without previous intention
or preparation, promptly, impulsively; to do something without
giving it a thought.

Cf. Straight from the shoulder.

452. РУБИТЬ СУК, НА КОТОРОМ СИДИШЬ

rubít' suk na kotórom sidísh

To be hewing down a bough on which you are sitting.

To act in such a way as to do oneself harm.

Cf. To cut one's own throat; to saw off the bough on which one is sitting.

453. РУКА НЕ ДРОГНЕТ

ruká n'e drógn'et

One's hand wouldn't shake doing something.

One won't hesitate to do something; one will do something without scruple.

Cf. One wouldn't think twice about doing something; without a qualm.

259

454. РУКА НЕ ПОДНИМАЕТСЯ

ruká n'e podnimáyetsa

One's hand won't rise.

One can't bring himself to do something;
one is hesitant about doing something.

Cf. Not to have the heart to do something.

455. РУКИ КОРОТКИ

rúki kórotki

One's hands are short.

One doesn't have
enough authority,
power or strength to
do something; one is
in no position to
do something.

**Cf. Just try! You couldn't
if you tried!**

456. **РУКИ НЕ ДОХОДЯТ**

rúki n'e dokhód'at

One's hands don't reach.

One has no time or possibility
to undertake something.

457. **РУКИ ЧЕШУТСЯ**

rúki chéshutsa

One's hands are itching.

Someone is anxious
to do something.

**Cf. One's fingers
/hands itch to do
something.**

458. РУКОЙ НЕ ДОСТАНЕШЬ

rukóy n'e dostán'esh

You can't reach someone with your hand.

Someone is out of reach
(usually said of someone in a high position).

459. РЫТЬ ЯМУ кому-либо

ryt' yámu

To dig a pit for someone.

To cause someone trouble;
to plunge into intrigue against
someone; to do someone harm.

Cf. To make/prepare a pitfall for someone.

C
460–537

460. САДИТЬСЯ НА ЛЮБИМОГО КОНЬКА

sadíttsa na l'ubímovo kon'ká

To mount one's favourite pony.

To dwell on one's favourite topic; to be on one's pet subject.
Cf. To mount/ride one's hobby/hobby-horse.

461. **САДИТЬСЯ НА ШЕЮ**

sadíttsa na shéyu

To sit down on someone's neck.

To submit someone to one's will; to put someone under one's complete control; to use someone as a tool.

Cf. To live off someone.

462. **САДИТЬСЯ НЕ В СВОИ САНИ**

sadíttsa n'e v svoí sáni

To get into someone else's sleigh.

To undertake to do something one knows nothing about or which one who has inadequate knowledge, training etc.; to occupy a post for which one is unsuited.

463. **САМИ С УСАМИ**

sámi s usámi

We too have a moustache of our own.

Not young in wisdom; no worse than.

Cf. We weren't born yesterday.

464. **САПОГИ ВСМЯТКУ**

sapogi vsm'átku

Soft-boiled boots.

Rot, nonsense, rubbish, a trifling matter, nothing.

465. СБРАСЫВАТЬ МАСКУ

sbrásyvat' másku

To throw off the mask.

To show one's true self, one's true character and intentions.

Cf. To throw off the mask.

466. СВЕТЛАЯ ГОЛОВА

sv'étlaya golová

A bright head.

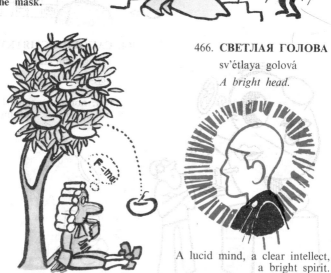

A lucid mind, a clear intellect, a bright spirit.

Cf. A clear head.

467. СВОДИТЬ КОНЦЫ С КОНЦАМИ

svodít' kontsý s kontsámi

To bring the ends together.

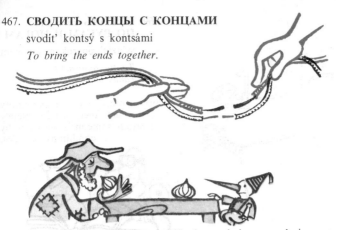

With great effort or difficulty to balance one's income with one's expenditures; to manage with one's resources.

Cf. To make both ends meet.

468. СВОРОТИТЬ ГОРЫ

svorotít' góry

To shift mountains.

To do something important which calls for great effort.

Cf. To move mountains. 267

469. СВЯЗАТЬ кого-либо ПО РУКАМ И НОГАМ

sv'azát' po rukám i nogám

To tie someone's hands and feet.

To deprive someone of the possibility to act freely; to completely restrain someone's activities by conditions or rules.

Cf. To bind/tie someone hand and foot.

470. СГЛАЖИВАТЬ ОСТРЫЕ УГЛЫ

sglázhivat' óstryye uglý

To smooth sharp corners.

To smooth things over; to relieve the situation; to ease tension; to adjust differences.

471. **СГОРАТЬ СО СТЫДА**

sgorát' so stydá

To burn with shame.

To feel great shame.

Cf. To burn with shame.

472. **СГУЩАТЬ КРАСКИ**

sgushchát' kráski

To thicken the paints.

To exaggerate; to picture something as being worse than it really is.

Cf. To lay it on thick.

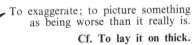

473. **СДАВАТЬ В АРХИВ**

sdavát' v arkhív

To relegate to the archives.

To dismiss as unfit for a particular use;
to bury in oblivion
as something obsolete or useless.

474. **СЕМЬ ПОТОВ СОШЛО**

s'em' potóv soshló

Seven sweats have come off.

One has exerted himself to the fullest
to accomplish something.

Cf. To sweat one's guts out.

475. СЕМЬ ПЯТНИЦ НА НЕДЕЛЕ

s'em' p'átnits na n'ed'él'e

Someone has seven Fridays in one week.

Someone who easily and frequently changes his mind, mood or intentions.

Cf. Someone is in twenty minds; to chop and change.

476. СЕРДЦЕ/ДУША НЕ ЛЕЖИТ
к чему-либо/кому-либо

sértse/dushá n'e l'ezhít

One's hear/soul doesn't lie for something or someone.

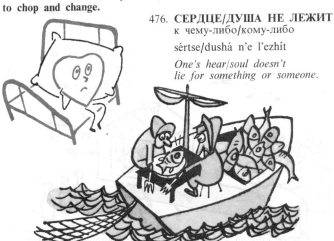

One feels no inclination toward something or someone; one has no liking for or confidence or interest in someone or something; one has a distaste for something.

271

477. СЕРДЦЕ/ДУША РАЗРЫВАЕТСЯ НА ЧАСТИ

sértse/dushá
razryváyetsa na chásti

One's heart/soul is breaking into pieces.

One feels great pity, compassion, grief;
one feels something keenly, takes
something hard.

Cf. One's heart is breaking.

478. СЕСТЬ В ЛУЖУ

s'est' v lúzhu

To sit down into a puddle.

To get oneself
into an awkward position or compromising situation;
to let oneself be duped; to do or say something stupid.

**Cf. To put one's foot in it;
to get oneself into a fix/spot.**

479. **СЕСТЬ НА МЕЛЬ**

s'est' na m'el'

To sit down on a shoal.

To get into an extremely difficult situation;
to be in unsatisfactory circumstances, especially with little money.

Cf. To be on the rocks; to be in low water; to be in a tight corner.

480. **СЖЕЧЬ КОРАБЛИ/МОСТЫ**

szhech korablí/mostý

To burn the ships/bridges.

To take an irrevocable step; to do something that makes it impossible to retreat, to change one's plans, etc.

Cf. To burn one's boats/bridges.

481. СИДЕТЬ МЕЖДУ ДВУХ СТУЛЬЕВ

sid'ét' m'ézhdu dvukh stúl'yev

To sit between two chairs.

To try to adhere to two different, irreconcilable points of view; to try to keep the favour of both sides in a dispute.

Cf. To run with the hare and hunt with the hounds; to play a double game.

482. СИДЕТЬ НА ЧЕМОДАНАХ

sid'ét' na chemodánakh

To sit on one's suitcases.

Packed and waiting to go.

483. СИДЕТЬ СЛОЖА РУКИ

sid'ét' slozhá rúki

To sit with one's arms folded.

To be idle; to sit still doing nothing.

Cf. To sit twiddling one's thumbs.

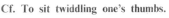

484. СКЛОНЯТЬ кого-либо ВО ВСЕХ ПАДЕЖАХ

sklon'át' vo vs'ekh pad'ezhákh

To decline someone in all the cases.

To talk a lot about someone at every opportunity (usually in a derogatory manner).

485. СКОЛЬЗИТЬ ПО ПОВЕРХНОСТИ

skol'zít' po pov'érkhnosti

To glide on the surface.

To deal with a subject only superficially; to pay attention to outward appearances without going to the root of the matter.

Cf. To skim the surface of something; never to go below the surface.

486. СКОЛЬКО ЛЕТ, СКОЛЬКО ЗИМ!

skól'ko l'et skól'ko zim

So many summers, so many winters!

How long ago! (A greeting used when two people haven't seen each other for a long time).

**Cf. Long time no see! I haven't seen you for ages!
Fancy meeting you after all this time.**

487. СЛАБАЯ СТРУНКА

slábaya strúnka

A weak string.

The most vulnerable aspect of someone's character;
a matter upon which one is easily affected or most sensitive.

Cf. A weak soft point.

488. С ЛЁГКИМ СЕРДЦЕМ

s l'ókhkim s'értsem

With a light heart.

Free from sorrow,
discomfort, anxiety,
misgivings.

**Cf. With a light
heart.**

489. С ЛЁГКОЙ РУКИ

s l'ókhkoy rukí

From the light hand of someone.

At someone's initiative or following someone's example
which set in motion a series of subsequent actions or deeds.

490. СЛЕД ПРОСТЫЛ

sl'ed prostýl

Someone's footprints have grown cold.

Someone has run away, disappeared;
there's not a trace of someone.

Cf. To vanish into thin air.

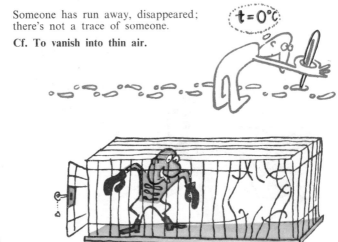

491. СЛОМАТЬ ЛЁД

slomát' l'od

To break the ice.

To put an end to formality, stiffness or shyness in one's relations with people; to make the first step; to mark the beginning; to cause any matter to start moving.

Cf. To start the ball rolling; to break the ice.

492. С ЛУНЫ СВАЛИЛСЯ

s luný svalíls'a

One has fallen from the moon.

Someone is puzzled; someone doesn't understand what is evident to everyone.

Cf. As if he were born yesterday; to fall from the moon. 279

493. **СЛЫШНО, КАК МУХА ПРОЛЕТИТ**

slýshno kak múkha prol'etít

One could hear a fly flying past.

It's absolutely quiet; it's deadly still.

Cf. You could hear a pin drop.

494. **СЛЮНКИ ТЕКУТ**

sl'únki t'ekút

Saliva is flowing.

Someone is anxious to partake of some tasty food or drink.

Cf. To make someone's mouth water.

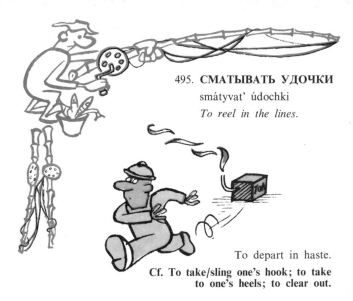

495. СМАТЫВАТЬ УДОЧКИ

smátyvat' údochki

To reel in the lines.

To depart in haste.

Cf. To take/sling one's hook; to take to one's heels; to clear out.

496. СМЕЯТЬСЯ В КУЛАК

sm'eÿattsa v kulák

To laugh into one's fist.

To laugh secretly to oneself while being outwardly serious.

Cf. To laugh in/up one's sleeve.

497. СМОТРЕТЬ В КОРЕНЬ

smotrét' v kór'en'

To look into the root.

To look deep into the matter; to investigate the matter thoroughly; to try to grasp the crux of a matter; to tackle something at its source.

Cf. To get to the heart/root of something.

498. СМОТРЕТЬ В ОБА

smotr'ét' v óba

To look through both.

To look attentively; to be closely observant; to be on the alert; to be particularly watchful.

Cf. To keep one's eyes peeled/skinned.

499. **СМОТРЕТЬ** кому-либо **В РОТ**

smotr'ét' v rot

To look someone in the mouth.

To listen attentively and servilely
to what one says; to fawn on someone.

Cf. To hang on someone's words.

500. **СМОТРЕТЬ ДРУГИМИ ГЛАЗАМИ**

smotr'ét' drugími glazámi

*To look at someone or something
with different eyes.*

To look at or assess someone or something in a different way.

Cf. To look with another eye upon.

501. СМОТРЕТЬ КАК БАРАН НА НОВЫЕ ВОРОТА

smotr'ét' kak barán na nóvyye voróta

To look at someone or something like a ram at a new gate.

To look at someone or something with a puzzled, perplexed or dismayed expression on one's face; to look rather stupid, not understanding what is going on; to look quite lost.

502. СМОТРЕТЬ СВЕРХУ ВНИЗ

smotr'ét' sv'érkhu vniz

To look down at someone from above.

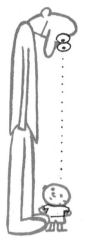

To regard someone as inferior or with disapproval; to treat someone haughtily, disdainfully.

Cf. To look down on someone; to look down one's nose at someone.

503. СМОТРЕТЬ СКВОЗЬ ПАЛЬЦЫ

smotr'ét' skvoz' pál'tsy

To look through one's fingers.

To purposely avoid seeing; to deliberately ignore a piece of misconduct or a transgression; to refuse to observe something; to connive at; to wink at.

Cf. To make light of; to turn a blind eye to; to look the other way; to look through one's fingers.

504. СМОТРЕТЬ СКВОЗЬ РОЗОВЫЕ ОЧКИ

smotr'ét' skvoz' rózovyye ochkí

To look through rose-coloured glasses.

Not to see a person's shortcomings; to take too optimistic a view of someone or something.

Cf. To view/look through rose-coloured glasses. 285

505. **СНИМАТЬ ПЕНКИ**

snimát' pénki

To skim.

To appropriate the best part of the results of someone else's labour.

Cf. To skim the cream off.

506. **СНИМАТЬ**
с кого-либо **СТРУЖКУ**

snimát' strúzhku

To take the shavings off someone.

To criticize someone
severely, to rate someone
soundly, to scold someone.

Cf. To tear someone off a strip.

507. **СНЯТЬ** перед кем-либо **ШЛЯПУ**

sn'at' shl'ápu

To take off one's hat before someone.

To express respect, admiration for a person's achievements.

Cf. To take off one's hat to someone.

508. **СОБАКУ СЪЕЛ**
на чём-либо

sobáku s'yél

*One has eaten
the dog at something.*

One has acquired great skill or experience in something;
one knows something thoroughly; one is an expert in something.

**Cf. To have something at one's fingertips; to know
something inside out; to know the ropes; he's been around.**

509. **СОВАТЬ НОС**
во что-либо

sovát' nos

*To stick one's
nose into something.*

To meddle in or interfere with other people's affairs;
to intrude where one is not wanted.

Cf. To poke/stick one's nose into something.

510. **СОН В РУКУ**

son v rúku

*The dream has come
into one's hand.*

Said of a dream that has come true.

511. СОРИТЬ ДЕНЬГАМИ
sorít' d'en'gámi
To litter with money.

To spend a large sum of money recklessly; to squander money.

Cf. To throw one's money about.

512. СО СКРИПОМ
so skrípom
With a creak.

To do something very slowly, with great difficulty or effort, reluctantly.

513. С ОТКРЫТОЙ ДУШОЙ/ С ОТКРЫТЫМ СЕРДЦЕМ

s otkrýtoy dushóy/
s otkrýtym s'értsem

With an open heart/soul.

To treat someone or do something sincerely, trustfully, frankly, openly, without prejudice.

514. СПАТЬ БЕЗ ЗАДНИХ НОГ

spat' b'ez zádnikh nog

To sleep without one's hind legs.

To sleep soundly.

Cf. To sleep like a log/top.

515. С ПЛЕЧ ДОЛОЙ

s pl'ech dolóy

Off one's shoulders.

One needn't bother about something any longer; one no longer has an irksome burden to bear; one has got rid of duties, cares, responsibilities.

Cf. That's done, thank goodness.

516. СПУТАТЬ ВСЕ КАРТЫ

spútat' vs'e kárty

To mix up all the cards.

To spoil or ruin someone's plans; to upset someone's calculations.

Cf. To upset someone's apple-cart.

291

517. СРАЖАТЬСЯ С ВЕТРЯНЫМИ МЕЛЬНИЦАМИ

srazhátsa s v'etr'anymi m'él'nitsami

To fight against the windmills.

To waste energy in combating imaginary evils or difficulties; to attack an imaginary foe.

Cf. To tilt at windmills.

518. СТАВИТЬ ВО ГЛАВУ УГЛА

stávit' vo glavú uglá

To put something in the vertex of an angle.

АНАТО-МИЯ

To assign primary importance to something; to consider something to be indispensible.

519. **СТАВИТЬ** кого-либо **НА НОГИ**

    stávit' ná nogi

    To put someone on his feet.

To cure someone of an illness.

520. **СТАВИТЬ НА ОДНУ ДОСКУ**

    stávit' na odnú dósku

    To put someone on the same board with someone else.

To put someone on the same level with someone else:
to consider one person comparable with another. 293

521. СТАВИТЬ что-либо С НОГ НА ГОЛОВУ

stávit' s nog ná golovu

To put something from its feet into its head.

To give a distorted picture of something; to put things in the wrong order; to take the effect for the cause.

Cf. To put the cart before the horse.

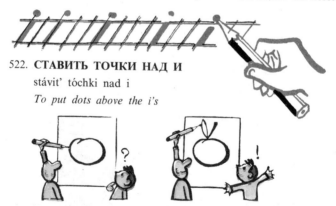

522. СТАВИТЬ ТОЧКИ НАД И

stávit' tóchki nad i

To put dots above the i's

To make something clear and definite; to give most careful attention to detail.

Cf. To put the finishing touches to something; to dot the i's and cross the t's.

523. СТАНОВИТЬСЯ НА ДЫБЫ

stanovíttsa na dybý

To stand up on one's hind legs.

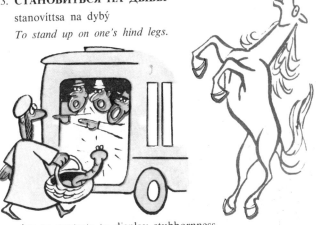

To resist; to protest; to display stubbornness.

Cf. To rear up; to stand up on one's hind legs.

524. СТАРО КАК МИР

staró kak mir

As old as the world.

Very old, stale, uninteresting because heard before.

Cf. As old as the hills.

525. СТИРАТЬ ГРАНИ

stirát' gráni

To grind off the edges.

To remove differences
or distinctions.

526. СТОИТ КАК ВКОПАННЫЙ

stoít kak vkópanny

One stands as if dug in.

One stands quite still,
motionless.

**Cf. To stand as if rooted
to the ground.**

296

527. **СТОЯТЬ** за кого-либо/что-либо
ГОРОЙ

stoyát' goróy

*To stand for someone
or something like a mountain.*

To defend someone or something
with all one's might, by every
possible means; to be solidly
behind someone or something;
to stand firm or stick up
for someone or something.

**Cf. To stand for someone
through thick and thin;
to back someone up to
the hilt.**

528. **СТОЯТЬ НАД ДУШОЙ**

stoyát nad dushóy
To stand over someone's soul.

To annoy someone by constantly
watching him; to importune
someone.

**Cf. To stand over someone;
to breath down someone's neck;
to worry the life out of someone.**

529. СТОЯТЬ ПОПЕРЁК ГОРЛА

stoyát' pop'er'ók górla

To stand across someone's throat.

To become unbearable, unendurable;
to be a source of annoyance,
irritation, especially a persistent one.

Cf. A thorn in one's flesh/side.

530. СТОЯТЬ ПОПЕРЁК ДОРОГИ

stoyát pop'er'ók dorógi

To stand across the road.

To be an obstacle, hindrance or impediment to someone; to hamper
someone's chances of success or progress.

Cf. To be/stand in someone's way.

531. СТРЕЛЯНЫЙ ВОРОБЕЙ

str'él'any vorob'éy

A sparrow that has been shot at.

A person experienced
in the matter at hand;
someone not easily deceived.

**Cf. An old hand;
a knowing old bird.**

532. СТРЕЛЯТЬ ИЗ ПУШКИ ПО ВОРОБЬЯМ

str'el'át' is púshki po vorob'yám

To fire a cannon at sparrows.

To use an instrument or take measures far more powerful
than is necessary; to make a great effort for a small gain.

**Cf. To use a sledge-hammer to crack a nut;
to break a fly/butterfly up on the wheel.**

533. СТРИЧЬ ВСЕХ ПОД ОДНУ ГРЕБЕНКУ

strich vs'ekh pod odnú gr'eb'ónku
To cut everyone's hair with one comb.

To treat everyone alike; to reduce everyone
to the same level; to judge all people
the same way.

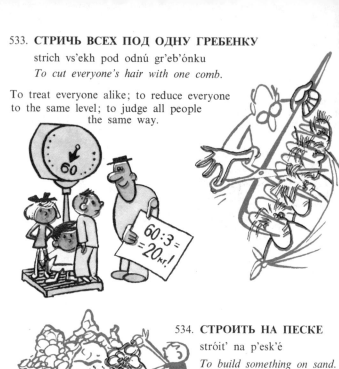

534. СТРОИТЬ НА ПЕСКЕ

stróit' na p'esk'é
To build something on sand.

To make plans,
organize a scheme,
etc., on an insecure
foundation,

Cf. To build on sand.

535. С ТЯЖЁЛЫМ СЕРДЦЕМ

s t'azhólym s'értsem

With a heavy heart.

To be anxious, depressed, in low spirits;
to have a presentiment that something unpleasant
or undesirable is about to happen.

Cf. With a heavy heart.

536. СЧИТАТЬ ВОРОН

shchitát' vorón

To count the crows.

To gape at something; to be distracted, inattentive; to be bored. 301

537. СЫТ ПО ГОРЛО

syt po górlo

Full right up to the throat.

One has had too much of something;
one is surfeited with something.

Cf. To be fed up with something; to have one's fill of something.

T

538–550

538. ТАНЦЕВАТЬ ОТ ПЕЧКИ

tantsevát' ot p'échki

To dance from the stove.

To begin with something that is elementary, familiar, or simpler, repeating all the movements or operations from the very beginning; to begin from the beginning.

539. ТАСКАТЬ КАШТАНЫ ИЗ ОГНЯ

taskát' kashtány iz ogn'á

To pull the chestnuts out of the fire.

To do the hardest and the most painstaking part of some job for someone else's benefit.

Cf. To pull the chestnuts out of the fire.

540. ТАЩИТЬ ЗА УШИ

tashchít' zá ushy

To pull someone by the ears.

To do everything to help someone (usually one who is remiss and of less than average ability) in his studies, in obtaining promotion, etc.

541. ТЁПЛОЕ МЕСТЕЧКО

t'óploye m'est'échko

A warm little place.

A highly paid appointment or job;
a profitable position.

Cf. A cushy/snug job.

542. ТЕРЯТЬ ГОЛОВУ

t'er'át' gólovu

To lose one's head.

To become flustered,
confused, panic stricken; to lose one's self-control.

Cf. To lose one's head/wits; to lose one's presence of mind.

543. ТЕРЯТЬ ПОЧВУ ПОД НОГАМИ

t'er'át' póchvu pod nogámi

To lose the ground under one's feet.

To lose self-confidence in one's occupation, social position or convictions.

Cf. To feel the ground slipping away from under one's feet.

544. ТИШЕ ВОДЫ, НИЖЕ ТРАВЫ

tíshe vodý nízhe travý

Quieter than water, lower than grass.

One is meek, timid, mild, quiet.

Cf. Quiet as a mouse; meek as a lamb.

545. ТОЛОЧЬ ВОДУ В СТУПЕ

tolóch vódu v stúp'e

To pound the water in the mortar.

To do useless work,
to engage in fruitless talk
that can have no results,
to waste time.

Cf. To beat the air; to mill the wind.

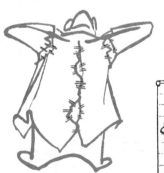

546. ТРЕЩАТЬ ПО ШВАМ

tr'eshchát' po shvam

To burst at the seams.

To be on the verge of destruction, collapse, ruin.

Cf. To go/fall to pieces; to fall/burst apart at the seams.

547. ТЯЖЁЛАЯ АРТИЛЛЕРИЯ

t'azhólaya artil'ériya

Heavy artillery.

Something that can be used in an emergency as an effective means of achieving an end.

548. ТЯЖЁЛ НА ПОДЬЁМ

t'azhól na pod'yóm

Heavy on the rise.

Slow or unwilling to do something; sluggish, hard to move or rouse to action.

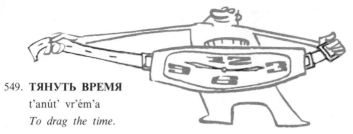

549. **ТЯНУТЬ ВРЕМЯ**

t'anút' vr'ém'a

To drag the time.

To be slow in acting; to procrastinate;
to wait for a favourable opportunity.

Cf. To bide one's time.

550. **ТЯНУТЬ ЗА ЯЗЫК**

t'anút' za yazýk

To pull someone by the tongue.

To make someone say something;
to pump someone.

У

551–565

551. **УБИТЬ ДВУХ ЗАЙЦЕВ**

ubít' dvukh záitsev

To kill two hares.

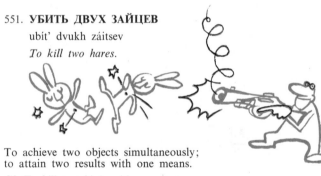

To achieve two objects simultaneously;
to attain two results with one means.

Cf. To kill two birds with one stone.

552. УДАРИТЬ КАК ОБУХОМ ПО ГОЛОВЕ

udárit' kak óbukhom po golov'é

To strike as if with an axe-butt on the head.

To amaze, to perplex, to stun someone; to take someone aback.

Cf. To knock someone down with a feather; to knock someone off his pins.

553. УДАРИТЬ ПО РУКАМ

udárit' po rukám

To strike each other's hands.

To confirm an agreement or a business deal; to strike a bargain.

Cf. To shake hands on it.

554. **УЗНАТЬ** что-либо **ИЗ ПЕРВЫХ РУК**

uznát' is pérvykh ruk

To learn something from the first hands.

To receive information direct from
a primary source without intermediaries.

Cf. At first hand.

555. **УЙТИ В КУСТЫ**

uytí v kustý

To go into the shrubs.

To withdraw from one's promise or an undertaking;
to disclaim further responsibility for something.

312 **Cf. To make oneself scarce; to back out; to show the white leather.**

556. УЙТИ В СЕБЯ

uytí v s'eb'á

To go into one's own self.

To become withdrawn,
uncommunicative;
to become less sociable and
more reserved.

**Cf. To retire into oneself;
to withdraw into one's shell.**

557. УЙТИ С ГОЛОВОЙ
во что-либо

uytí z golovóy

To go headlong into something.

To be fully absorbed, deeply engrossed or totally involved in something.

**Cf. To throw oneself/plunge into something;
to get up to one's neck in something.**

558. УКАЗАТЬ кому-либо
НА ДВЕРЬ

ukazát' na dv'er'

To point to the door.

Peremptorily to ask a person, whose presence is unwelcome, to leave the house, room, etc.

Cf. To show someone the door.

559. УМЫВАТЬ РУКИ

umyvát' rúki

To wash one's hands.

To divest oneself of any

further connection
with or responsibility
for something; to abandon the matter entirely.

Cf. To wash one's hands of something.

560. УНОСИТЬ НОГИ

unosít' nógi

To carry away one's legs.

To flee; to run as fast as one's legs will carry one; to have a narrow escape.

Cf. To escape by the skin of one's teeth.

561. УПАСТЬ С НЕБА НА ЗЕМЛЮ

upást' s n'éba na z'éml'u

To fall from the sky to the earth.

To be disillusioned; to abandon fantasy and return to practical realities.

Cf. To come down to earth. 315

562. УСТРАИВАТЬ СЦЕНУ

ustráivat' stsénu

To make a scene.

To start a noisy or violent argument, quarrel or scrap
with someone, expressing one's dissatisfaction, irritation, etc.

**Cf. To stage/kick up a row;
to make a scene.**

563. УТЕРЕТЬ
кому-либо **НОС**

ut'er'ét' nos

*To wipe someone's
nose.*

To win an advantage over someone; to humiliate or cause
disgruntlement; to make a clever retort.

**Cf. To score off someone; to get the better of someone;
to steal a march on someone.**

564. УХО РЕЖЕТ

úkho r'ézhet

Something cuts one's ear.

It's grating upon one's ears; it's painful to listen to; it offends the ear.

565. УШИ ВЯНУТ

úshy v'ánut

One's ears fade.

It is so ridiculous, absurd or silly that it's disgusting to listen to.

Cf. It makes one sick to hear about it.

X

566–576

566. **ХВАТАТЬ ЗВЁЗДЫ С НЕБА**

khvatát' zv'ózdy s n'éba

To snatch the stars from the sky.

To be very good at something;
to be able to do something remarkable.

Cf. He is as good as they come.

567. ХВАТАТЬСЯ ЗА ГОЛОВУ

khvatáttsa za gólovu

To clutch one's head.

To be struck with horror;
to abandon oneself to despair.

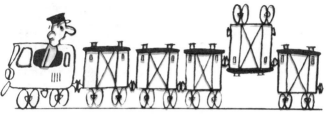

568. ХВАТАТЬСЯ ЗА СОЛОМИНКУ

khvatáttsa za solóminku

To clutch at a straw.

When in extreme danger, difficulty, etc.,
to try to seize any chance,
however small or useless, of getting out of it.

Cf. To catch/clutch at a straw.

569. ХОДИТЬ ВОКРУГ ДА ОКОЛО

khodít' vokrúg da ókolo

To walk round and about.

To avoid saying something openly, frankly, directly;
to avoid the essential facts; not to come to the point;
to approach a matter in a roundabout way.

Cf. To beat about the bush.

570. ХОДИТЬ НА ГОЛОВЕ

khodít' na golov'é

To walk on one's head.

To get into mischief;
to play pranks; to be naughty (usually said of children).

571. ХОДИТЬ ПО КРАЮ ПРОПАСТИ

khodít' po kráyu própasti

To walk on a brink of an abyss.

To be in imminent mortal danger;
to be on the verge of disaster.

Cf. On a brink of a precipice.

572. ХОДИТЬ ПО СТРУНКЕ

khodít' po strúnk'e

To walk on a string.

To be completely under someone's authority;
to be very obedient, almost to the point of servility.

**Cf. To be at someone's beck and call;
to dance attendance upon someone; to toe the line.** 321

573. ХОТЬ ТРАВА НЕ РАСТИ

khot' travá n'e rastí

Who cares whether or not the grass grows.

One couldn't care less; it's all the same to someone.

Cf. Not to care a straw.

574. ХОТЬ ШАРОМ ПОКАТИ

khot' sharóm pokatí

You could even roll a ball through it.

There's nothing there; it's completely empty.

Cf. Bare as a bone; as bare as the palm of one's hand.

575. ХРОМАТЬ НА ОБЕ НОГИ

khromát' na ób'e nogí

To limp on both legs.

To have serious gaps in one's knowledge, training or abilities.

576. ХУДОЙ КАК СПИЧКА

khudóy kak spíchka

Thin as a matchstick.

Very thin.

Cf. Thin as a lath/rake.

Ц

577

---

577. **ЦЕНЫ НЕТ**
кому-либо/чему-либо

tsený n'et

*There's no price on
someone or something.*

Someone or something
is priceless, invaluable.

Ч

578–586

578. **ЧЕРЕЗ** чью-либо **ГОЛОВУ**

chér'ez gólovu

Over someone's head.

To do something without informing
one's immediate superior;
to apply to a higher authority
by passing an intermediate one.

Cf. To go over someone's head.

579. ЧЕРЕЗ ЧАС ПО ЧАЙНОЙ ЛОЖКЕ

chér'ez chas po cháynoy lózhk'e
One teaspoonful every other hour.

To be few and at long intervals; very slowly.

Cf. In drops; in/by driblets; few and far between.

580. ЧЁРНАЯ КОШКА ПРОБЕЖАЛА

chórnaya kóshka prob'ezhála
A black cat has run between them.

There's a coolness between them;
they have become estranged.

Cf. They have fallen out.

581. ЧЁРНЫМ ПО БЕЛОМУ

chórnym po b'élomu

In black on white.

To declare or state something definitely, clearly, distinctly.

Cf. In black and white.

582. ЧЁРТОВА ДЮЖИНА

chórtova d'úzhina

A devil's dozen.

Thirteen.

Cf. A devil's/a baker's dozen.

583. **ЧЕСАТЬ ЯЗЫК**

chesát' yazýk

To scratch one's tongue.

To engage in idle talk; to talk continuously; to chatter.

Cf. To wag one's tongue.

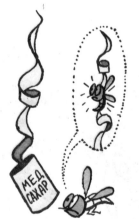

584. **ЧИТАТЬ МЕЖДУ СТРОК**

chitát' m'ézhdu strok

To read between the lines.

To discern the concealed meaning; to draw conclusions which are not obvious in something said or written.

Cf. To read between the lines.

585. ЧУДЕСА В РЕШЕТЕ

chud'esá v r'eshet'é

Miracles in a sieve.

It's amazing,
incredible, unbelievable,
extraordinary; it's
a fantastic tale.

586. ЧУЖИМИ РУКАМИ ЖАР ЗАГРЕБАТЬ

chuzhími rukámi zhar zagr'ebát'

To bank up the fire with someone else's hands.

To benefit by the results
of someone else's work;
to use the results

of someone else's work to achieve one's selfish ends.

**Cf. To make a cat's-paw of someone; to pull
someone's chestnuts out of the fire.**

Ш

587–590

587. **ШАПКАМИ ЗАКИДАЕМ**

shápkami zakidáyem

*We'll pelt you (him, etc.)
with our caps.*

We expect to win without difficulty; it's as good as certain
(to boast of an easy victory).

330 **Cf. It's a walk-over; it's in the bag.**

588. ШАПОЧНОЕ ЗНАКОМСТВО

shápochnoye znakómstvo

A cap acquaintance.

A slight acquaintance.

Cf. A nodding/bowing acquaintance.

589. ШИТО БЕЛЫМИ НИТКАМИ

shíto b'élymi nítkami

It is sewn with white thread.

It is a flimsy story or excuse
easily seen through; it is all too obvious;
it is quite transparent.

**Cf. Something does not
hold water; made up out
of whole cloth.** 331

590. ШУТКИ В СТОРОНУ

shútki v stóronu

Jokes aside.

Speaking seriously;
it's serious matter;
let's get down to business.

**Cf. Joking apart/aside;
all kidding aside.**

591–594

591. **ЯБЛОКУ НЕГДЕ УПАСТЬ**
   yábloku n'égd'e upást'
   No room for an apple to fall.

Used to indicate that there is a large number of people
in one place, that the place is overcrowded, that there is
hardly room to move or turn around.

Cf. There's no room to swing a cat.

592. ЯЗЫК СЛОМАЕШЬ

yazýk slomáyesh

You can break your tongue.

It's very difficult to pronounce a word or a phrase.

Cf. You can break/twist your tongue.

593. ЯЗЫК ХОРОШО ПОДВЕШЕН

yazýk horoshó podv'éshen

One's tongue is hung well.

Someone is a·smooth talker; someone has a glib tongue.

Cf. To have the gift of the gab.

594. ЯСНО КАК ДЕНЬ

yásno kak d'en'

Clear as a day.

Easy to see or comprehend;
quite evident, obvious; as plain or clear as can be.

Cf. As plain as the nose on your face; as plain as day.

344

Марк Исаакович Дубровин

Русские фразеологизмы в картинках
(*для говорящих на английском языке*)
Издание 2-е, исправленное и дополненное

Редакция учебников и учебных пособий
для зарубежных школ

Зав. редакцией Л. В. Матвеева
Редактор Н. Н. Кузнецова
Редакторы английского текста Р. Ньюнэм, Е. Г. Коненкин
Мл. редактор Н. И. Максакова
Художник В. И. Тильман
Художественный редактор Г. И. Петушкова
Технический редактор С. С. Якушкина
Корректор О. М. Зудилина